Women in Higher Education Administration

Adrian Tinsley, Cynthia Secor,
Sheila Kaplan, *Editors*

NEW DIRECTIONS FOR HIGHER EDUCATION

MARTIN KRAMER, *Editor-in-Chief*

Number 45, March 1984

Paperback sourcebooks in
The Jossey-Bass Higher Education Series

Jossey-Bass Inc., Publishers
San Francisco • Washington • London

Adrian Tinsley, Cynthia Secor, Sheila Kaplan (Eds.).
Women in Higher Education Administration.
New Directions for Higher Education, no. 45.
Volume XII, number 1.
San Francisco: Jossey-Bass, 1983.

New Directions for Higher Education Series
Martin Kramer, *Editor-in-Chief*

New Directions for Higher Education (publication number USPS
990-880) is published quarterly by Jossey-Bass Inc., Publishers.
New Directions is numbered sequentially — please order extra
copies by sequential number. The volume and issue numbers
above are included for the convenience of libraries. Second-class
postage rates paid at San Francisco, California, and at
additional mailing offices.

Correspondence:
Subscriptions, single-issue orders, change of address notices, undelivered
copies, and other correspondence should be sent to Subscriptions,
Jossey-Bass Inc., Publishers, 433 California Street, San Francisco,
California 94104.

Editorial correspondence should be sent to the Consulting Editor,
Martin Kramer, 2807 Shasta Road, Berkeley, California 94708.

Library of Congress Catalogue Card Number LC 83-82747

International Standard Serial Number ISSN 0271-0560

International Standard Book Number ISBN 87589-995-1

Cover art by Willi Baum

Manufactured in the United States of America

Ordering Information

The paperback sourcebooks listed below are published quarterly and can be ordered either by subscription or as single copies.

Subscriptions cost $35.00 per year for institutions, agencies, and libraries. Individuals can subscribe at the special rate of $25.00 per year *if payment is by personal check.* (Note that the full rate of $35.00 applies if payment is by institutional check, even if the subscription is designated for an individual.) Standing orders are accepted.

Single copies are available at $8.95 when payment accompanies order, and *all single-copy orders under $25.00 must include payment.* (California, Washington, D.C., New Jersey, and New York residents please include appropriate sales tax.) For billed orders, cost per copy is $8.95 plus postage and handling. (Prices subject to change without notice.)

Bulk orders (ten or more copies) of any individual sourcebook are available at the following discounted prices: 10–49 copies, $8.05 each; 50–100 copies, $7.15 each; over 100 copies, *inquire.* Sales tax and postage and handling charges apply as for single copy orders.

To ensure correct and prompt delivery, all orders must give either the *name of an individual* or an *official purchase order number.* Please submit your order as follows:

Subscriptions: specify series and subscription year.
Single Copies: specify sourcebook code and issue number (such as, HE8).

Mail orders for United States and Possessions, Latin America, Canada, Japan, Australia, and New Zealand to:
Jossey-Bass Inc., Publishers
433 California Street
San Francisco, California 94104

Mail orders for all other parts of the world to:
Jossey-Bass Limited
28 Banner Street
London EC1Y 8QE

New Directions for Higher Education Series
Martin Kramer, *Editor-in-Chief*

Contents

Editors' Notes

This *New Directions for Higher Education* sourcebook is about the careers of women in higher education administration. It discusses the career paths that women follow, the barriers that women face as their careers develop, the barriers that minority women face, what can be done to encourage women to enter higher education administration, what can be done to help them to gain senior positions, and how our institutions can benefit once women hold senior positions in proportion to their numbers in the profession.

This book is for practitioners—it is for women who want to advance in the profession of higher education administration and for senior women who can help newcomers progress. It is also for senior managers—male and female—who have responsibility for developing and maintaining the vitality of their institutions and who must therefore identify, train, and nurture talented staff. Finally, it is for everyone who is concerned with the future of higher education in this country—college and university administrators, members of boards of trustees, representatives of higher education associations, state and national policy makers, and foundation officers.

The editors of this volume and the authors of its chapters have all been involved in activist projects to advance women in higher education administration. We have been guided in these efforts by a number of assumptions and beliefs. First, higher education institutions can be greatly improved by the addition of women and minorities to the pool from which leaders are drawn. We know from experience that the best-managed institutions—those most creative, dynamic, and responsive to change—are committed to and supportive of the advancement of women and minorities. We also believe that institutions that do not make use of the skills of women and minorities are wasting enormous talent and potential.

Second, senior administrators should be concerned with expanding the pool of talented women and minorities who can serve their institutions. To that end, they should offer increased responsibility and the possibility of upward mobility, and should monitor progress, provide timely criticism and

The editors gratefully acknowledge the support provided by a Mina Shaughnessey Fellowship from the Fund for the Improvement of Post-Secondary Education. Named for the late Mina Shaughnessey, author of *Errors and Expectations* (New York: Oxford University Press, 1977), and funded by the Carnegie Corporation and the Fund for the Improvement of Post-Secondary Education, these fellowships provide higher education practitioners and others involved in projects directed toward change in higher education and toward social change with time in which to reflect on their work and make their experience available to others.

advice, and recognize the contributions that women and minorities make to the vitality of their institutions. We believe the identification, development, and management of talented subordinates is the most important function of senior management.

Third, women and minorities who hold senior positions have a special obligation to assist others who aspire to leadership roles. We believe that on the whole, women and minorities accept the responsibility to encourage and support younger people.

Fourth, male administrators and male-dominated boards of trustees must redouble their efforts to recruit and support women administrators in the 1980s and 1990s. Although the last fifteen years have seen some progress, significant backsliding is possible if this issue is not kept high on the list of institutional priorities.

Finally, individual careers always unfold within an institutional context. The more fully an individual understands the relation between his or her aspirations and ambitions, the institution's formal and informal agendas, and the expectations and norms of higher education, the more likely that individual will be to achieve and advance. In addition, as senior officers come to understand the normal career patterns in higher education, the normal routes to substantive responsibility, and the normal barriers and obstacles, they become better able to advise and work with women and minorities, whose careers do not always unfold in the normal ways.

This volume is timely for several reasons. First, only during the last several years have empirical studies analyzing the career paths of university administrators been completed. Thus, we now have a data base that permits us to make a longitudinal comparison of the careers of male and female administrators. Second, more than a decade has passed since organized efforts to improve the status of women and minorities in higher education administration began. The Project on the Status and Education of Women — the first national clearinghouse for information about women in education — was established at the Association of American Colleges in 1971. The Office of Women in Higher Education was established at the American Council on Education in 1973. Higher Education Resources Services (HERS) offices were established in New England in 1972, in the Mid-Atlantic region in 1975, and in seven western states in 1979. This sourcebook profiles some programs developed by these offices. Third, all these projects have depended for funding on foundations and government agencies supportive of equity issues. As grant funding from these sources runs out, there is a danger that interest in and support for the advancement of women and minorities in higher education will decline. Since so much of the agenda remains unfinished, it is timely to remind the profession of what has been accomplished during the past decade and to tally what remains to be done.

In Chapter One, Kathryn Moore draws on data from the Leaders in

Transition project to describe what we know about women's careers and the ways in which they differ from those of men. Moore uses national data to develop and describe the elements that define careers in higher education for both men and women.

In Chapter Two, Adrian Tinsley provides a conceptual framework for the professional development of higher education administrators and offers a detailed description of career mapping—a structured exercise that allows one to analyze one's work situation and set goals for moving ahead. This career-planning exercise has proved extremely helpful to those who have used it. The concepts outlined in this chapter have also been helpful to administrators responsible for developing and evaluating professional staff.

Chapter Three, by Cynthia Secor, and Chapter Four, by Jeanne Speizer, explain the format and content of programs designed to provide women administrators with professional skills, knowledge of organizational structures, and familiarity with current issues in higher education administration—areas thought to be crucial to advancement. Chapter Three describes the Summer Institute, a three-and-one-half week program held each July at Bryn Mawr College and co-sponsored by HERS, Mid-America and Bryn Mawr. Chapter Four examines the Administrative Skills Program, five weekend seminars held each year at Wellesley College and sponsored by HERS, New England. Chapter Four also evaluates the difference that attending a skills training program can make in a woman administrator's career.

In Chapter Five, Donna Shavlik and Judy Touchton write the history of the National Identification Program, which was established in 1977 by the Office of Women in Higher Education at the American Council on Education and which now operates in all fifty states. The National Identification Program has two goals: to identify talented women and work to enhance their opportunities for advancement, and to isolate barriers to progress for women and develop ways of removing them.

The concept of networking—the idea of promoting contacts among women, and among women and men, for the purpose of sharing information, advice, and professional help—informs all the projects described in this volume. In Chapter Six, Margaret Wilkerson describes the distinctive barriers that minority women face and the networks that they have developed. Wilkerson also addresses the connection between the use of networks for personal advancement—a legitimate need and desire—and as part of a collective effort to provide many with the opportunity for advancement.

In Chapter Seven, Sheila Kaplan and Dorothy O. Helly discuss the special obligations of senior women to women administrators, faculty, and students. They suggest an agenda that senior women can pursue, and they identify some barriers to its accomplishment. In Chapter Eight, Alison Bernstein discusses the principles that foundations follow in providing start-up money to projects aimed at expanding the pool of leaders available to higher education institutions. Finally, in Chapter Nine, the editors review the barriers and blocks that inhibit the advancement of women and minorities in higher education administration and the strategies that have been developed to overcome them.

Adrian Tinsley
Cynthia Secor
Sheila Kaplan
Editors

Adrian Tinsley, associate vice-chancellor for academic affairs in the Minnesota State University System, designed the professional development unit for the Bryn Mawr/HERS Summer Institute for Women in Higher Education Administration, where she serves as faculty in residence.

Cynthia Secor, founding director of HERS, Mid-Atlantic, which for many years was based at the University of Pennsylvania, continues in this role with HERS, Mid-America, which is based at the University of Denver. She is cofounder and codirector of the Summer Institute for Women in Higher Education Administration.

Sheila Kaplan, former vice-president for academic affairs at Winona State University and former director of the City University of New York baccalaureate program, is vice-chancellor for academic affairs in the Minnesota State University System.

The organization of institutions of higher education has created
a career structure that clusters women in pockets or tracks at the
bottom of many career ladders.

Careers in College and University Administration: How Are Women Affected?

Kathryn M. Moore

Women are achieving leadership positions in postsecondary education today. Since 1972, there has been a small but steady increase in the number of women appointed to top posts. For example, the American Council on Education reports a ten-year gain of more than a hundred women presidents. Many of the new appointments are in the public coeducational universities and in community colleges, where women have not been selected before (Taylor, 1981).

The research on women in administration has also increased dramatically in the past ten years, both in quantity and in quality. New and important studies of women administrators address such issues as minorities (Jackson, 1983); types of institutions, including both two-year and four-year settings (Heming, 1982; Taylor, 1981); regions of the country (Ironside, 1983); and positions most often occupied by women (Estler and Miner, 1981; Moore and Sagaria, 1981). All these studies have increased and refined our knowledge of women's careers and their institutional contexts.

In examining the overall status of women in administration, the tendency is to concentrate on the absence of women from leadership positions rather than on the contributions that women in such positions have made.

A. Tinsley, C. Secor, S. Kaplan, (Eds.). *Women in Higher Education Administration.*
New Directions for Higher Education, no. 45. San Francisco: Jossey-Bass, March 1984.

But, much can be learned from the successful women (and men) who now occupy top positions. The Leaders in Transition project was initiated in 1981 to construct a national profile of college administrators. Nearly 3,000 individuals representing fifty-five positons were surveyed at 1,400 four-year institutions. The project's findings provide important national data on the career paths of college and university administrators — a subject that received very little systematic attention in the past. These data allow us to compare the career paths of male and female administrators on a national basis.

The Demographics of Administration

The Leaders in Transition project was funded by the Pennsylvania State University, the Ford Foundation, and the Exxon Educational Foundation through a grant to T.I.A.A.-C.R.E.F. The twenty-nine-item survey questionnaire used in the project was developed at the Center for the Study of Higher Education at Pennsylvania State University. The stratified random sample of line administrators in accredited four-year degree-granting institutions consisted of approximately 4,000 administrators at 1,600 institutions. The sample was further stratified by position type as described in the 1979-80 Educational Directory. Thus, such generic titles as president, provost, vice-president, registrar, and dean were included, and assistant and associate titles, except for assistant to the president, were excluded. The response rate was 71 percent.

Professional Background. To enable researchers to analyze the career paths of administrators accurately, respondents were asked to list all paid professional positions that they had held, beginning with their current position, each institution of employment, and the dates during which they held each position. They were to include any part-time, jointly held, or acting positions.

The total number of professional positions held ranged from one to seventeen. To establish a workable data base, no more than ten positions were coded for any one individual. The number of professional jobs that most respondents had held fell within a range of three to eight.

Current Position by Race and Sex. Of the 2,896 senior administrators who responded to the survey, an overwhelming 91.8 percent were white, 5.4 percent were black, and 2.8 percent represented other racial or ethnic groups. There was a higher percentage of black women administrators than black men — 8 percent and 4.8 percent, respectively. Among representatives of the other racial or ethnic groups, there were three times as many males as females. For purposes of analysis, respondents in the "other" category were grouped with blacks to form a joint category called *minority.*

When the sample was analyzed by sex, we found that 577 respondents — 20 percent of the total — were women. As Table 1 shows, the three administrative positions that employed the largest number of women were head librarian, registrar, and director of financial aid. The same three positions also contained the largest number of minority administrators. For male respondents, the three top positions were president or chancellor, chief business officer, and registrar.

Of the 653 deans or directors in the sample located at twenty-nine different academic schools or colleges, 13.8 percent were women. The field for more than half of the women deans was nursing, home economics, arts and sciences, or continuing education, and there were no women deans of business, engineering, law, medicine, or physical education. Minority deans or directors of academic units represented 5.5 percent of the total. The greatest concentration was in education.

These data illustrate two critical issues in administrative careers. The first issue is the matter of career tracks. For each top position in academic administration, a series of more or less standard positions precedes it. These career tracks or families usually include distinguishable administrative functions, such as student personnel services, business affairs, alumni affairs, or academic affairs (Van Alstyne and others, 1977). It is commonly believed that, once launched in a given track, individuals do not move easily to another. Job requirements and credentials can be so distinctive within a track that lateral mobility is difficult.

The second issue is that women and minorities seem to be able to build careers in some tracks more easily than in others. Some career tracks, such as student personnel, appear to be quite hospitable to women and minority group members, while others, such as academic affairs, have almost no representation from these groups. Moreover, certain types of institutions appear to offer more opportunities than others do. Hence, women and minorities can become pocketed in career tracks or positions, which makes subsequent career mobility difficult.

First Person to Hold Position. To trace the rapid expansion of new jobs at many colleges and universities over the past few decades, we asked respondents to indicate whether they had been the first person to occupy any

Table 1. Distribution of Male and Female Administrators by Current Position

	Male		Female		Total	
	N	Percent	N	Percent	N	Percent
Presidents	149	90.6%	13	9.4%	162	100%
Provosts	133	86.4	21	13.6	154	100
Academic deans	563	86.2	90	13.8	653	100
Registrars	142	71.7	56	28.3	198	100
Librarians	121	65.8	63	34.2	184	100
Student affairs	133	80.1	33	19.9	166	100
Alumni	47	56.6	36	43.4	83	100
Financial aid	98	64.5	54	35.5	152	100

of their paid positions. The results showed that 18 percent had been the first person to hold their position. White males were more likely to hold new positions than minorities or women were. We might expect this trend to have reversed in recent years, because affimative action policies encourage the filling of new positions with women and minorities, but data from the Leaders in Transition project as well as other research (Dingerson and others, 1980) suggest that it has not.

Length of Time in Current Position. Most of the senior officials surveyed had held their current position for five years or less. In 1981, 53 percent had begun their current position in 1976 or later. When length of time in current position was analyzed by gender, it was found that the percentage of women who had held their position for five years or less was slightly higher than the percentage of men. For instance, approximately 32 percent of the women had been in office for one or two years, compared with 22 percent of the men. In contrast, approximately 47 percent of the men had held their current position for six or more years, compared with 34 percent of the women.

Type of Institution Where Currently Employed. The Carnegie Code Classification System identifies three major types of four-year institution: research universities, comprehensive universities and colleges, and liberal arts colleges. When the distribution of female and minority administrators was analyzed by type of institution, the differences were striking. Liberal arts institutions employed the largest number of the 577 female administrators who responded—60.5 percent of the total—compared with 30.3 percent of the males. The largest percentage of male respondents was found in the comprehensive universities and colleges—45.6 percent. Although these institutions were collectively the second largest employer of women respondents, the proportion of women employed at these institutions fell to 29.6 percent of the total female sample. The predominance of women administrators in liberal arts colleges extended to the chief executive level: Eight of the thirteen women presidents in the sample were chief executive officers of liberal arts institutions.

When type of control was examined, the number of male respondents currently employed at public and private four-year institutions was fairly evenly divided. Slightly more than half of the men—51.8 percent—were employed at a public college or university, and just under half—48.2 percent—were at private institutions. In sharp contrast, the majority of female administrators—71.8 percent—was found at private colleges. Only 28.2 percent were employed in public institutions.

Private institutions employed 53.6 percent of the white administrators, while public institutions employed 46.4 percent. The reverse was true for minority administrators: Somewhat more than half—58.3 percent—were employed by colleges or universities, while 41.7 percent worked at private institutions. It seems clear that women and minorities have fared best in the institutions designed to serve them, that private education has been the most responsive to women, and that the reverse has been true for minorities.

Educational Background. As another means of tracking the career paths of college administrators, we asked respondents to list their earned degrees. Nearly half of the males in the sample—49.3 percent—listed three earned degrees, compared with one third of the female respondents—33.5 percent. Slightly less than one third of the women in the sample—32.4 percent—had acquired the doctorate, while more than half of the men—52.3 percent—had earned this degree.

For both minorities and whites, the majority had acquired three degrees—46.3 percent of the whites and 44.1 percent of the minorities. The figures for those with two degrees were again nearly equal—33 percent of the white respondents and 34.9 percent of the minorities. Few administrators—13.9 percent of the whites and 12.4 percent of the minorities—had only one earned degree. For both sexes and both race categories, the Ph.D. was the most common doctoral degree: 71.7 percent of the women, 66.4 percent of the men, and 56.5 percent of the minorities held the Ph.D.

Personal Background. Administrators in our sample ranged in age from twenty-four to seventy-four. Nearly one third were between forty-five and fifty years old. Minority administrators displayed patterns characteristic of their sex. Seventy-nine percent of our respondents were married and living with their spouse. However, there were clear differences in marital status by sex. Twice as many male as female administrators were married and living with their spouse. Far more women than men were single by virtue of membership in a religious order—15 percent and 2.4 percent, respectively. No minority administrator was in a religious order, and 7.5 percent had never been married.

Spouses' Occupation. For the spouses of the 2,033 married male administrators in our sample, 39.8 percent were homemakers. The two next largest categories were educational occupations (including primary and secondary schoolteachers and counselors) and clerical occupations. Only 4.2 percent of the wives were college professors, and only 2.5 percent were college administrators. For the spouses of our 251 married female respondents, 17.9 percent were employed as college professors, and 11.2 percent were college administrators. The next largest occupational area among spouses of women administrators was business and management—23.9 percent. This figure includes the self-employed and consultants. An additional 19.5 percent were professionals—lawyers, psychologists, and journalists.

Elements That Define Careers in Administration

What other elements besides gender and race shape administrative careers? To answer this question, we must first define *career.* As I define the college and university administrative career, it is a series of jobs involving tasks of governance and management that tends over time to increased responsibility, reward, and recognition. While this is only a working definition, it makes explicit a number of elements that help to explain our observations of careers in college and university administration.

For administrative careers, successive or multiple positions are an essential element of my definition, as is a hierarchy of positions. Careers have direction. The usual metaphor for a career is a ladder, and people usually think of climbing up ladders, not down them. The metaphor is apt, because it incorporates the ideas of direction, steps or rungs, and fixed points of entry and exit—bottom and top. It is believed that the number of administrative positions at colleges and universities has increased; hence, the hierarchy itself has expanded in recent years.

Time is another element of administrative careers. Time span is the length of an individual's entire career. Frequently organizations set time limits that serve as floors and ceilings for careers, such as entry after college at age 20 or older, and final exit or retirement at age 70 or earlier (but seldom later).

The most common measure of time employed within careers is time in position. In some occupations time accrued in position is called tenure and results in a specific set of contractual conditions. In other occupations time accrued in position results in seniority. Time in position can be multiplied by the number of positions held to yield a notion of speed. By this route, we can distinguish careers that are fast-track from careers that are slow-track or stuck. That is, some individuals rise through the positions in a hierarchy at a rapid clip and achieve a top position at a relatively young age. Other individuals rise through the same hierarchy at a slower pace. Some never reach the top. Some business organizations, such as those studied by Kanter (1977), develop and use fast track career routes to train and test promising young executives. There appears to be little deliberate career structuring in academe, but some individuals still find ways of reaching top positions rapidly.

Still another element of careers is the positions or jobs themselves. As White (1970) and others have demonstrated, positions often have histories. This is notably true of the college or university presidency, but it is true of other administrative positions as well. New occupants often learn that they have inherited a legacy of debts and credits from past holders of the position (Kauffman, 1980).

It is sometimes assumed that the ladder to top positions includes a finite set of positions through which an individual must move: for example, assistant dean to associate dean to dean. But, as most observers of academe know, the hierarchies in higher education are seldom as rigid as they are in other organizations, such as the military or the civil service.

Administrators not only change positions, the positions that they occupy themselves evolve. For example, the position of dean can retain the same title for many years while it alters dramatically in scope or organizational location (Estler and Miner, 1981). Some people are skilled at extending the positions that they occupy. Other people change positions when they outgrow them.

Administrative careers in higher education are shaped by the organizations that compose the marketplace, but they do not depend on any one college or university. In contrast, administrative positions are highly dependent on the organization in which they are located. Even the position of president — which we seem to understand the best — receives its essential dimensions from the college or university in which it is found. No presidency is exactly like another, primarily because of the organizational context.

Careers in administration can and do extend beyond or across single organizations, but positions do not. In this regard, administrative careers differ somewhat from careers in other professions, such as law or medicine. As Gross and McCann (1983) and others have shown, academic administration appears to be unusual in that it is common to bring in someone from outside when top positions, especially the presidency, need to be filled. Other administrative positions tend to rely on loyal insiders, even alumni, but these positions are often support positions, such as dean of student affairs or director of alumni affairs (Marlier, 1982). These facts are relevant to our discussion of career tracks: It is important to distinguish the ladders that rely the most heavily on insiders from those that rely on outsiders, especially for top leadership posts.

This analysis of the elements of administrative careers would not be complete without attention to the three Rs: responsibility, recognition, and reward. Implicit in the notion of career ladder is the idea that successive positions involve increasing responsibility, demand greater skill, and confer greater rewards and status. These elements are not perfectly linked. We can all think of positions whose rewards are out of line with their scope of responsibility or visibility, and women usually know which way the misalignment works. But, in the ideal career these elements align with the rank that the position occupies in the career track.

Personal Characteristics That Shape Careers in Administration

Findings from other research help to define the reality that shapes administrative careers for women. These findings relate to three personal characteristics: age, marital status, and doctoral education.

Age. Despite legal and other impediments, organizations in general have tended to discriminate on the basis of age. Colleges are no different: On the one hand, the system is based on seniority but on the other, the system favors youth (Rosenbaum, 1979).

A few years ago, Mary Ann Sagaria and I studied the careers of more than 600 college administrators in Pennsylvania, including both line and staff positions (Sagaria and Moore, forthcoming). Generally speaking, we found a preference for youth, but there were some interesting variations for women. For example, upward career mobility tapered off for men after age fifty to fifty-five, but mobility appeared to increase for women of the same age. We attributed a large part of the increase for women to the effect of affirmative action policies that encouraged institutions to discover and promote some of their senior women.

When the Leaders in Transition data on age distributions were plotted by sex, we discovered an interesting skew in the proportions of males and females by age. At ages twenty to twenty-nine, the proportions of men and women were nearly equal. For ages thirty-to thirty-nine, there were two males for every female; for ages forty to forty-nine, there were four males for every female; for ages fifty to fifty-nine, there were three males for every female; and for ages sixty to sixty-five, there were two males for every female. These data suggest two things about the career possibilities for men and women. First, it seems likely that mobility among the age cohorts will continue to exhibit a preference for youth and that most jobs will go to men. But, because there are so few women among the ranks of forty- and fifty-year-olds, any move by a women will receive a lot of attention, and it is likely to be perceived as a gain for all women. Second, women in the ranks of the thirty- forty-, or fifty-year-olds have to compete less with other women for any given position than they do with men, because in most cases there will be more male than female candidates.

Marital Status. Many of us have wondered how the idea developed that women's marital status inhibits their professional mobility. Fewer than 50 percent of the women administrators in the Leaders in Transition survey were married. Moreover, research by Curby (1980) suggests that most women desire mobility and that they are willing to change institutions, cities, and even states in order to get a better job. Why, then, does the myth persist that women are not mobile because they are married?

The Leaders in Transition study points to an answer: Almost 90 percent of the male respondents were married, more than half to homemakers. When these married male respondents were asked whether spouse or family considerations would be important in making a subsequent move, the majority said no. Is it possible that male administrators who appear to have traditional marriages project their own marital attitudes onto women colleagues? Do they assume that most women are married because most men are, and do they also believe that women should take the family situation into account, although they themselves do not need to?

It is true, of course, that the professional women who are married are likely to be married to another professional. The needs of dual career couples are real. But, not all women are married—indeed, fewer than half are—and each woman's circumstance deserves to be considered on her own terms, not by the institution's assumptions about her circumstances.

Doctoral Education. Leaders in Transition data and other studies of administrators' careers lead to two conclusions about doctoral-level education (Gross and McCann, 1983). First, a doctorate is the baseline credential for all positions in college administration above entry level. Approximately 50 percent of the Leaders in Transition respondents held the doctorate. However, fewer than 30 percent of the female respondents did. Women (and others) are disadvantaged if they lack the doctorate, even when competing for the many entry-level administrative positions in today's market. Women seeking top positions should realize that 80 percent of all presidents and provosts hold the doctorate and that 90 percent of the women in such positions have it. Second, 13 percent of the Leaders in Transition study respondents had degrees in higher education and educational administration. These degrees have sometimes been disparaged as not sufficiently academic. Overall, education degrees are held predominately by women and minority group members.

Organizational Factors That Affect Careers in Administration

The third component of a career is the organization. Idiosyncratic as colleges and universities are, they provide the context in which people build administrative careers. Individual administrators are not entirely free to pick and choose among positions. Rather, each institution establishes the positions and chooses the individuals to occupy them in intricate ways. Institutions can do many things to create a pool of candidates for their positions. Policies and procedures can be designed to reduce, expand, enrich, or impoverish that pool. Until affirmative action policies came into being, the matter seems not to have been well understood; certainly, it was not systematically organized.

As the data on distribution of men and women by age cohorts cited earlier show, colleges and universities can take actions that determine the kinds of people who can become candidates. Policies can be set to affect the distribution of women. Affirmative action guidelines are designed to do this in a positive way. Other policies can have an indirect but negative effect on women. In the past, antinepotism rules often prevented spouses, who were usually female, from working on the same campus as their partners.

One way of examining the equity issue for women in administration is by analyzing where women are located in their organizations. At present, women are pocketed. When it comes to principal line administrators, such as those studied in the Leaders in Transition project, women are pocketed in one kind of institution, the liberal arts college. Moreover, more than 70 percent of all women are pocketed in private colleges, although most women students attend public colleges.

Women are also pocketed in certain positions. Survey data indicate that they are to be found primarily as registrars, librarians, and student affairs officers. They compose only 19 percent of the academic deans, and the majority of the women in this position head units in only three fields: nursing, home economics, and continuing education.

Finally, women are pocketed in sectors of their colleges and universities that make them less likely to build administrative careers. Faculty have traditionally been the pool from which administrative talent has been drawn, but women faculty are still scarce, especially at senior levels. Women are plentiful in the clerical and technical areas, but colleges and universities have erected fairly impermeable barriers between these areas and the higher levels of administration.

Conclusion

Today, both institutions and their administrative personnel are far more complex and sophisticated than they ever were before. It seems likely that many, if not most, institutions do not fully understand their own career structures. Movement among positions is often uneven, nonstandard, and noncomparable. Status, opportunity, and reward are not always effectively linked. Nevertheless, the administrative function continues to expand in colleges and universities. The demand placed on administrators to perform new and more intricate tasks increases, and the need for competent, committed individuals to perform these tasks will not diminish.

The Leaders in Transition survey shows that women are not distributed evenly across all categories of institutions or positions. Rather, they are clustered in pockets at the bottom of many career ladders. The definition of administrative career discussed in this chapter suggests that many elements combine to form a career in administration and that colleges and universities play a controlling, structuring role in the definition, duration, and outcome of administrative careers. Such personal characteristics as age, marital status, and educational credentials, combined with gender, tend to differentiate the typical career paths of women administrators from the typical paths followed by male counterparts. These career paths and opportunity structures deserve further study and discussion.

For the present, let us acknowledge that women administrators, whether they will it or not, are engaged in a struggle to preserve and expand the opportunities for other women. This struggle deserves the best efforts of their male colleagues as well, since the vitality and future viability of our nation's colleges and universities depend on it.

References

Curby, V. M. "Women Administrators in Higher Education: Their Geographic Mobility." *Journal of the National Association of Women Deans, Administrators, and Counselors,* 1980, *44* (1), 1–10.

Dingerson, M. R., Rodman, J. A., and Wade, J. F. "The Hiring of Academic Administrators Since the 1972 Higher Education Guidelines." *Research in Higher Education,* 1980, *13,* 9–22.

Estler, S., and Miner, A. S. "Towards a Model of Evolving Jobs: Professional Staff Mobility in the University." Paper presented to the American Education Research Association, Los Angeles, April 1981.

Gross, E., and McCann, J. C. "Careers of Academic Administrators in the U.S.A.: An Approach to Elite Study." *Research in Sociology of Education and Socialization,* 1983, *2,* 127–162.

Heming, R. M. "Women in Community College Administration: A Progress Report." *Journal of the National Association of Women Deans, Administrators, and Counselors,* 1982, *46,* 3–8.

Ironside, E. "Women as Administrators in Higher Education." Paper presented to the Association for the Study of Higher Education, Washington, D.C., March 1983.

Jackson, R. *Minority Administrators in Higher Education.* Washington, D.C.: American Council on Education, 1983.

Kanter, R. M. *Men and Women of the Corporation.* New York: Basic Books, 1977.

Kauffman, J. E. *At the Pleasure of the Board: The Service of the College and University President.* Washington, D.C.: American Council on Education, 1980.

Marlier, J. D. "Factors Relating to the Extent of Inbreeding Among College and University Administrators." Unpublished doctoral dissertation, Pennsylvania State University, 1982.

Moore, K. M., and Sagaria, M. A. "Women Administrators and Mobility: The Second Struggle." *Journal of the National Association of Women Deans, Administrators, and Counselors,* 1981, *44,* 21–28.

National Center for Education Statistics. *Educational Directory, Colleges and Universities, 1979–80.* Washington, D.C.: National Center for Education Statistics, 1979.

Rosenbaum, J. E. "Organizational Career Mobility: Promotion Changes in a Corporation During Periods of Growth and Contraction." *American Journal of Sociology,* 1979, *85,* 21–48.

Sagaria, M. A., and Moore, K. M. "Job Change and Age: The Experience of Administrators in Colleges and Universities." *Sociological Spectrum,* forthcoming.

Taylor, E. "Women Community College Presidents." In J. S. Eaton (Ed.), *Women in Community Colleges.* New Directions for Community Colleges, no. 34. San Francisco: Jossey-Bass, 1981.

Van Alstyne, C. J., Withers S., Mensel, R. F., and Malott, F. S. *Women and Minorities in Administration of Higher Education Institutions: Employment Patterns and Salary Comparisons.* Washington, D.C.: College and University Personnel Association, 1977.

White, H. *Chains of Opportunity.* Cambridge, Mass.: Harvard University Press, 1970.

Kathryn M. Moore is associate professor and research associate at the Center for the Study of Higher Education at Pennsylvania State University.

Career mapping can heighten one's sense of readiness for increased responsibility and suggest new possibilities for a professional career.

Career Mapping and the Professional Development Process

Adrian Tinsley

The research on women's careers in higher education (Moore, 1982; Capek, 1982) tells us that higher education has a pyramidal structure and that women are clustered at the bottom. Women are more likely to be assistants to, assistants, or associates than they are to be directors, deans, vice-presidents, provosts, or presidents. Women are more likely to be staff than line. In college and university administration, the three positions most often held both by women and by minorities are registrar, librarian, and director of financial aid (Moore, 1982). Research also shows (Moore, 1982; Frances and Mensel, 1981) that most women administrators do a great deal of "women's work" in higher education administration: They hold positions in continuing education programs that focus on women or reentry women. They run programs that deal with women or minorities as a special constituency, such as women's studies programs, women's resource centers, developmental skills centers, and special advising centers. They serve as deans of professional programs in which students are primarily women, such as nursing, home economics, and social work programs (Bennett, forthcoming).

Like their male counterparts, able, ambitious women administrators need opportunities to move up in the administrative hierarchy to positions that are more complex, demanding, powerful, and rewarding. Women who have learned or sharpened their managerial skills in programs that serve women

A. Tinsley, C. Secor, S. Kaplan, (Eds.). *Women in Higher Education Administration.*
New Directions for Higher Education, no. 45. San Francisco: Jossey-Bass, March 1984.

and minorities need opportunities for mainstream administrative service in arenas where their work will have an impact on the institution as a whole.

The Summer Institute for Women in Higher Education Administration, cosponsored by Higher Education Resource Services (HERS), Mid-America and Bryn Mawr College, was designed to provide women administrators with skills that can enhance their performance in their present positions and to give them insights into the institutional structure of higher education that can help them to move ahead.

Every year since 1976, a group of seventy to eighty women faculty and administrators committed to a career in higher education administration has attended the Summer Institute. These women come from all areas of higher education. They are faculty and department chairs, assistant deans, and deans. They are in the academic vice-president's office or assistant to the president. They are affirmative action officers, deans of students, directors of counseling centers, development officers, registrars, librarians, physical plant directors, business managers, and food service managers. They are sufficiently ambitious to commit nearly four weeks to a residential skills training and professional development program. Most are sufficiently well placed on their campuses to receive institutional support to attend. All are sufficiently experienced in higher education to be admitted to the program.

The curriculum at the Summer Institute focuses on management and leadership skills, finance and budget, accounting, administrative uses of the computer, governance, law in higher education, collective bargaining, and a variety of policy issues in higher education administration. The Summer Institute is fully described in Chapter Three. Here, we will concentrate on its professional development curriculum. From the beginning, professional development has been central to the experiences offered to Summer Institute participants.

In working with individual faculty and administrators, we attempted from the outset to be clear about the outcome that could be expected from the professional development process. We defined professional development as activity leading to increased knowledge and competence in one's present position or to enhanced qualifications for a more responsible position. Both are legitimate outcomes. In the second case, advancement is the goal, and career is viewed as a series of increasingly complex, responsible, and rewarding jobs. In the first case, advancement is not the goal. Rather, professional development is seen as enhancing or enlarging one's present job.

In the early years, the professional development unit included information on resumé construction and interviewing techniques, discussion of career goals and career problems in small-group settings, and encouragement to participants to talk about their career goals with one another in the context of their personal and professional life settings. As we gained more experience with the curriculum, we began to see that we could also teach techniques for the analysis of institutional structures. An individual's career always unfolds in an institutional setting. A career in higher education unfolds in institutions that have relatively rigid norms and traditions and quite particular histories, behavioral expectations, problems, and ways of solving problems. The more fully an individual can understand the relation between her aspirations and ambitions and her institution's formal and informal agendas and the more fully she can understand the relation between her personal values and needs and her institution's organizational structures and political processes, the likelier it becomes that she will achieve and advance.

When women who attend the Summer Institute are asked to name the obstacles that they are aware of in pursuing their careers, they list them in this order: lack of experience, lack of education, personal or family responsibilities, and lack of mobility. I am not inclined to dismiss the statements that women themselves make about the perceived obstacles. Educational credentialling, for example, is a real issue. The doctoral degree remains extremely important for advancement in higher education administration, yet less than one third of all women administrators hold it, compared with more than half of the male administrators. Issues related to mobility and personal or family responsibilities are also real. In higher education, advancement usually requires a geographical move, which can be highly disruptive to the family structures and personal support networks of both married and single women. A women's decision to seek advancement is made in the context of personal values, needs, and obligations as well as in the context of professional goals and ambitions.

However, individual women can take steps to identify and address the obstacles to advancement that they perceive in their own situations, whether these obstacles are personal or professional. What we have come to call career mapping is a structured exercise that helps women to articulate their personal values and professional ambitions and to develop strategies to overcome the barriers to advancement that may be present. For the individuals with whom we have worked, career mapping has increased their energy for pursuing a career, no matter how they define that career.

There are two tools for an analysis of the individual's personal and professional setting: the resumé and the organization chart. Analysis involves a set of parallel questions to be asked simultaneously about the individual and the organization.

The Individual

1. What are my goals?

2. What bars me from achieving my goals? Education? Experience? Mobility? Personal or family responsibilities? Other barriers?

The Organization

1. What is the mission of my institution?

2. What bars my institution from moving me toward my goals? Its values? Traditions? Structures? External constraints? My experience in

the institution? My reputation? My visibility? My centrality to the institution's mission? Its informal agendas?

How can I get around these barriers?
Is it worth it to do so?

3. What conflicts might I experience in achieving my goals?

Conflicts with the people in my life (spouses, children, parents, lovers, friends)? Internal conflicts (personal value conflicts, time and energy commitment required for advancement)?

Conflicts with my institution? With people (colleagues, superiors, people who work for me, people in other departments or units)? Conflicts with institutional structures? With external forces that affect the institution?

How can I resolve or harmonize these conflicts?
Is it worth it to me to do so?

4. What resources do I bring to achieving my goals?

Education? Experience? Mobility? Ambition and drive? Resources that come from the people in my life?

Resources that come from my institution? From colleagues, subordinates, superiors? From my unit or structures outside my unit? From institutional needs? Formal or informal agendas? Financial resources that my institution can invest in me?

In career mapping, the task is to articulate personal values and career goals in an institutional context and from an institutional perspective, to understand not simply one's own job or department or division but the institution as a whole, its mission, its values, its context in higher education nationally and locally, its informal agendas, its resources, and its problems. The point of the task is to enable the individual to work more effectively within the institution, to advance within it, to change it — or to leave it.

The questions just listed represent a short form of the professional development exercises that we use at the Summer Institute. Here, they highlight the fact that one must work back and forth between one's own situation and the institution's situation, recognizing the full complexity of both. Higher education administrators in general — whether they are women or men — are not accustomed to analyzing their careers in a personal time frame with special attention to personal rewards and costs, defining the skills and resources needed for job enrichment and career mobility, or extending their perspectives on higher education in general and on their own institutions in particular.

In a complete career-mapping exercise, the individual is asked to use whatever written form is personally comfortable — essay, chart, map with annotations, graphic — to develop an action plan for her own career, beginning with present title and salary and a brief description of present responsibilities and projecting title, salary, and responsibilities along the following time line: one year from now, two to three years from now, and at retirement. Most people think of a number of reasons why they do not want to do this, why they should not have to do this, and why they cannot do this. Reasonable people differ in the extent to which they believe that careers can be planned or that they happen serendipitously. Nevertheless, many participants report that having to think through these issues in writing is the most important outcome of their work at the Summer Institute.

Participants also are asked to indicate the points at which they see conflicts in their action plans. These conflicts can be personal, or they can arise from their situation within their institution. Finally, they are asked to project alternative career scenarios contingent on alternative events in their personal and professional lives. As in all planning efforts, the close-in projections are the most realistic. As the projections get further out, one has increasing license to be speculative about what one really wants.

A number of questions help women to clarify their thinking about careers in higher education:

Value Questions

Do I expect to be working for most of my life?

Do I expect to work regardless of what else I may do?

What do I really want to achieve? What is really most important in my life?

Situational Questions

Is my personal situation likely to support or impede whatever it is that I really want to achieve?

Is my institutional situation likely to support or impede whatever it is that I really want to achieve?

What do I expect to be happening for women in the United States in the time frame that I am projecting?

What do I expect to be happening politically, economically, socially, technologically in the United States in the time frame that I am projecting?

What do I expect to be happening in higher education in the time frame that I am projecting?

Questions to Ask About the Next Significant Job

What is the next significant job that I want to hold?

When do I want it?

Where is it?

What kind of experience does it require? What kind of knowledge base? What skills? What credentials?

Are there any jobs that I must hold in between? How do I get them, and when?

What people will be involved in helping me to get the job that I aim for?

Will state, local, or national networks be of help? Will professional associations be of help? Can women's networks help me?

Are there issues on my campus now that will affect my ability to get the next job that I want? What are they? Will they affect my goals? My career?

Are there issues important to minorities that will affect my ability to get the next job that I want? What are they? Will they affect my goals? My career?

Where can I take my career plan for realistic feedback? For help?

More Value Questions

When they give me the gold watch, how do I really want to be remembered, judged?

When I look back, what do I really want to have achieved?

After completing the career-mapping exercises, Summer Institute participants meet in groups of three to discuss them. Then, each triad meets with a person chosen for her broad experience in higher education administration and for her ability to listen well. As triad members talk with one another, the outside expert becomes less important. We have found over the years that triad members themselves provide one another with the personal support that is needed to examine barriers and conflicts, and usually they take responsibility for addressing those issues for each group member. The expert is most useful when she provides information about professional development resources and validates tentative expressions of ambition: "In my judgment, yes, you are ready for a deanship now."

The value of performing the career-mapping exercise in the Summer Institute context is the range of contacts that participants can make across a variety of jobs and types of institutions. In campus-based settings, one has the opportunity to connect across the usual divisional lines. When the exercise is done in informal friendship groups, it can provide continuing professionally oriented personal support. When it is done individually, it can be scary but still useful — like making a will. And, like a will, it needs to be updated every few years, as situations and goals change.

The triad or other small group can also provide useful follow-up to the career-mapping exercise. At the end of the Summer Institute, we ask each participant to review her analysis of her current position and her career map and choose three goals that — given her present job situation — would do the most to increase job effectiveness, career prospects, or both. For each goal, participants list one or two specific actions to be taken immediately, within six months, and within a year. If people are interested in thinking beyond their own careers to higher education in general, particularly if they are interested in thinking about higher education's hospitality to women and minorities, we ask them to identify goals related to making higher education a better place in which to work and a better place in which to learn and to list specific actions to be taken immediately, within six months, and within a year. We ask triads to keep in touch on a regular basis. As with any support group, a telephone call to ask how the plan is progressing can be a help.

As already noted, we define professional development as activity leading to increased knowledge and competence in one's present position or enhancing one's qualifications for a more responsible position. What outcomes do we expect from career mapping and from conscious attention to the professional development process? These are some of the measurable outcomes that we can expect to see: job change (advancement) within one's field, increased responsibilities on the present job, enhanced ability to work across divisional boundaries, participation in continuing education, completion of a degree, commencement of work on a new degree, participation in internships or job rotation, publication, increased involvement with networks of women in higher education, increased involvement with professional associations in higher education, and career change (to a different field). We believe that these are the right outcome measures. They measure whether we have achieved our goals of enabling the individual to work more effectively within the institution, to advance within it, to change it — or to leave it.

We can also expect to see increased ability to articulate career goals, raised aspirations, and increased energy for pursuing a career. At the Summer Institute, we see participants' sense of self-worth heightened (probably as a result of the opportunity to compare themselves with peers). There is also a heightening in their sense of readiness for increased responsibility and in their sense of the possibilities for a professional career. Their ability to analyze an institution's mission, organizational structure, resources, and constraints increases. Their ability to analyze their own position, their formal and informal power, their reputation, and the value of their job to the institution increases. And, their understanding of the problems facing higher education and the possibility of helping to solve those problems at their own institutions also increases.

Most women end the Summer Institute with an increased commitment to their work in higher education, often because — despite the problems — it offers the clearest pathway to a professional life that is consonant with their personal values. Some women end the Summer Institute with the knowledge that their professional opportunities will be significantly greater in other fields, and they leave higher education. In each case, there is greater clarity about professional goals, the prospects for achieving them, and the relation between goals and personal values and needs.

To return to the question of whether a career can be planned or whether it develops by accident and chance, the career-mapping exercise does not assume that a professional life (or that life in general) can be plotted on a two-, five-, or ten-year curve. It does assume that careers, like lives, have a shape and that different aspirations, needs, possibilities, and constraints shape them at different times. Both career mapping and the articulation of what one wants from one's personal and professional life are energizing. If an individual can reason or feel her way into the curve of her own personal and professional life, if she can articulate it and make it conscious, if she can understand the institution and the enterprise in which she works, she will be able to take the normal accident and chance of daily personal and professional life and shape it in a way that is consonant with what she most genuinely desires.

References

Bennett, S. K. "Women in Higher Education Administration: Prospects and Institutional Policy Response in the 1980s." In T. M. Stauffer (Ed.), *Political Controversies on Campus: The Making of Higher Education Policy.* Lexington, Mass.: Lexington Books, forthcoming.

Capek, M. E. *Higher Education Administrators in New Jersey: A Preliminary Report on Research Findings.* Princeton, N.J.: Princeton University in cooperation with the American Council on Education, 1982.

Frances, C., and Mensel, R. F. *Women and Minorities in Administration of Higher Education Institutions: Employment Patterns and Salary Comparisons 1978–79 and an Analysis of Progress Toward Affirmative Action Goals 1975–76 and 1978–79.* Washington, D.C.: College and University Personnel Association, 1981.

Moore, K. M. *Leaders in Transition: A National Study of Higher Education Administrators.* University Park, Penn.: Center for the Study of Higher Education, Pennsylvania State University, 1982.

Adrian Tinsley, associate vice-chancellor for academic affairs in the Minnesota State University system, designed the Professional Development Unit for the Bryn Mawr/HERS Summer Institute for Women in Higher Education Administration, where she serves as faculty in residence.

*Women who wish to advance in higher education need expertise
both in managing its administrative and governance structures
and in managing their own careers.*

Preparing the Individual for Institutional Leadership: The Summer Institute

Cynthia Secor

The Summer Institute for Women in Higher Education Administration has
proved to be one of the most enduring and visible of the professional development activities pioneered in the mid 1970s. Cosponsored by Bryn Mawr
College and HERS, Mid-America (formerly HERS, Mid-Atlantic), the Summer Institute is a four-week residential program held each July on the Bryn
Mawr college campus. It began in 1976 with funding from the William H.
Donner Foundation. In its third year, the Summer Institute became fully self-
supporting, and it remains so to this day.

The goal of its founders was to improve the status of women in the middle and executive levels of higher education administration, areas in which
women have traditionally been underrepresented. Now in its ninth year, the
Summer Institute accepts women faculty and administrators who are actively
seeking increased administrative responsibilities, and it provides them with
training in academic governance, finance and budgeting, management and
leadership, administrative uses of the computer, human relations skills, and
professional development; an institutional perspective on the pressing issues
and problems of higher education; strategies for professional development,
with special emphasis on leadership, human relations skills, and career map-

A. Tinsley, C. Secor, S. Kaplan, (Eds.). *Women in Higher Education Administration.*
New Directions for Higher Education, no. 45. San Francisco: Jossey-Bass, March 1984.

ping; and a continuing support network of peers, sponsors, and mentors. Since 1976, 579 women faculty and administrators from the United States, Canada, Sweden, Wales, Iran, Nigeria, and the Netherlands have participated in the program.

Assumptions of the Seventies

At its inception, the Summer Institute represented a state-of-the-art response to the issues of the 1970s. Women were absent from leadership positions, even from middle management positions, in institutions of higher education. Ruth Oltman's 1970 study of American Association of University Women corporate members demonstrated a conspicuous absence of women in the administrative ranks (Tinsley, 1975). A National Education Association report on the status of women administrators and faculty for the years 1971–72 confirmed the pattern (Tinsley, 1975). The Carnegie Commission Report on Opportunities for Women in Higher Education (1973) stated: "If women are thinly represented in faculties, especially in the traditionally male fields, they are so rarely represented in top academic administrative positions as to be practically nonexistent" (p. 123).

At the same time, women showed an avid interest in higher education administration. The Eastern Regional Conference for Women in Higher Education Administration, which was held at Princeton University in May 1975 under the cosponsorship of HERS, Mid-Atlantic, Princeton University, and the New Jersey chapter of the National Organization for Women drew 800 women. Many were given release time and a travel subsidy to attend a conference whose stated aim was to develop informal networks of communication among women administrators that could facilitate professional development.

Institutions appeared to be willing to support professional development activities for women as a concrete way of demonstrating their stated commitment to affirmative action. The founders of the Summer Institute believed that institutions would hire and promote women if institutional officers could be shown that women were ready and available for advancement. The major strategies that had emerged by the mid 1970s were to identify women, link them with one another and with concerned men, and provide intensive training when appropriate. Academic women were already in the work force. It remained to give them access to institutional resources and to remove institutional barriers.

The founders of the Summer Institute made two central assumptions about the competencies that women who wished to advance in higher education administration needed. First, they needed expertise in managing the administrative and governance structures peculiar to higher education. Second, they needed expertise in planning and managing a career in institutions where for the most part they had been either invisible or unnaturally visible by virtue of their token status.

In retrospect, it is significant that the work of the seventies focused both on the advancement of individuals and on the building of formal and informal advocacy groups that would ensure over time the advancement of women as a class. The original proposal to the William H. Donner Foundation spoke of training women in administrative and management skills, but significantly it identified as its principal long-term goal the development of a network of women administrators who would have both the skills and the motivation to improve the employment situation of other women on their campuses and in their regions.

Creation of the Summer Institute

In the mid 1970s, the William H. Donner Foundation sought to move women into management in all sectors of society. Its officers believed that the inclusion of women in the management of higher education would enrich the leadership of higher education in the United States and Canada. It was to the Donner Foundation that Bryn Mawr College and HERS, Mid-Atlantic turned for support, arguing that a partnership between the two institutions would result in a program of national stature. Bryn Mawr College had a long and distinguished history of educating women, and a training program cospon-sored and housed by the college could be expected to meet the standards of excellence for which the college was well known. HERS, Mid-Atlantic had as its charge the advancement of women employed in higher education. It was systematically involved in professional development activities and in the crea-tion of a communications and support network for academic professional women. Bryn Mawr College and HERS, Mid-Atlantic believed that their co-sponsorship would give a unique cast of tradition and innovation, education and advocacy to the proposed Summer Institute. Their respresentatives argued that the inclusion of a professional development sequence in the management curriculum would provide the learning experience most needed by the concerned, ambitious professionals whom they sought to serve. Plan-ning became the focus of the curriculum. The Summer Institute would begin with an introductory unit on governance and institutional planning and end with a unit on life and career planning. This comfortable union of the public and the personal, the institutional and the individual has become the hallmark of the Summer Institute experience.

From the outset, the commitment of the Summer Institute was to a residential educational experience in the liberal arts tradition that would allow a carefully selected group of women to live and study together; to selection of faculty for their academic training, administrative experience, and commit-ment to the advancement of women; and to a comfortable facility that allowed for study, recreation, and reflection. The founding directors were active in both women's studies and adult education, and they felt that it was their respon-sibility to provide a stimulating environment in which experienced adult professionals could learn from lecturers, case studies, simulations, readings, tapes, and conversation with staff, faculty, and other participants. Peer learning was to be a major part of the experience, and to this end the participant group was to be varied.

The Summer Institute was designed to serve women. Its founders knew that women professionals face personal and institutional barriers to advancement that their male colleagues do not share. Socialization leads women professionals to articulate values and adopt administrative and leadership styles that differ somewhat from those of male colleagues. It seemed essential for women to have an opportunity to talk freely about these and other issues. The founders took it for granted that the faculty would consist of both women and men. Participants were to benefit from observing a wide spectrum of management styles. They would also benefit from the experience of a wide variety of educational leaders. However, the majority of faculty would be women, who could serve both as sources of information and as professional role models.

Developing the Curriculum

The Summer Institute curriculum was designed to meet the challenge laid down by a member of the HERS, Mid-Atlantic Advisory Committee who was a college president. When asked to send a member of her staff, she hesitated. "I can teach her most of these skills here at the college," she said, "but can you teach her to think beyond her department, to think in terms of the needs of the institution as a whole?" That is what the curriculum was designed to do.

Sixty-seven women attended the first Summer Institute in 1976. In addition, twenty-six attended a special leadership seminar for women associate deans, deans, vice-presidents, provosts, and presidents, and thirty-four attended another special seminar on career development. These two satellite seminars were designed to enrich the networking process. Each satellite seminar had its own program and shared some faculty and social activities with participants in the core program.

For the core participants, the curriculum covered six major areas: financing of higher education; the academy as employer; administrative uses of the computer; planning for the institution and the individual; professional networks, support systems, and mentor relations; and decision making and the economic matrix. Learning was experiential, affective, and participatory. Participants engaged in case studies, supervised off-campus consulting, case writing, simulations, and small-group discussions in addition to lectures and assigned readings.

In every sense, the curriculum and the learning environment replicated the vital and somewhat chaotic academic women's movement of the period. The women learned much, lasting bonds were formed, faculty were enthusiastic, and staff emerged exhausted, gratified, and sobered by the scope and complexity of the venture that they had launched. However, some problems were obvious. The design of the institute was too complex. The participants at the two seminars and in the core group had good experiences, but there was not enough time to mingle the three groups effectively. The satellite seminars were dropped from subsequent institutes. The preparation of case studies about career development and academic administration proved too complex an activity to be done in conjunction with the rest of the curriculum. The cases were subsequently written by the HERS, Mid-Atlantic staff with support from a second William H. Donner Foundation grant.

Although staff were highly skilled and dedicated, they were too few in number to meet the demands of a residential program that placed its diverse participants in an unusually intense learning and living situation. Staff were added in subsequent years to conduct small-group work devoted to human relation skills, such as listening, conflict management, and group building.

The founders' concern for affirmative action needed to be present in the curriculum in concrete ways. Thus, work on higher education and the law was added at subsequent institutes, and the presentations on collective bargaining and professional development were refined to include specific actions that could be taken to improve the employment status of women and minorities. Although minority women were fairly well represented among participants, the curriculum of the first institute did not address the concerns and experience of minority people systematically. Moreover, staff and faculty were not representative of the minority professionals working in higher education. As a result of the institute's commitment to minority concerns, minority participation was increased to roughly 20 percent, minority faculty and staff were added, and issues of particular concern to minority administrators were added to the curriculum.

Refining the Curriculum

The Summer Institute curriculum has remained dynamic, changing in response to the extensive evaluations prepared by each successive class. However, a core curriculum has been developed, which now includes information and training in six areas: professional development, academic governance, human relations skills, finance and budgeting, administrative uses of the computer, and management and leadership.

Professional Development. The unit on professional development was conceptualized in the second year, and it continues to provide the distinctive flavor of the Summer Institute. The focus is on individual career mapping, the creation of professional networks, and the analysis of institutional environments. A series of lectures is closely coordinated with this unit. Lectures address such public policy issues as access to new technology, the future of women's colleges, the future of traditionally and historically black colleges, and the future of public higher education. This unit continues to be the locus of presentations about minority experiences. Considerable emphasis is placed on understanding the differences created by race, ethnic background, urban or rural environments, life-styles, faculty or other professional socialization, marital status, educational credentialing, and the other social and professional variables that can divide us and distance us from one another.

Academic Governance. The unit on academic governance focuses on the decision-making process, policy implementation, and constituent groups. It explains the complex mixture of collegiablity, bureaucracy, and politics that characterizes the management of higher education. Attention is given to the unique opportunities and constraints that characterize multicampus systems, research universities, private liberal arts colleges, church-related institutions, and community colleges. The role of the trustee is explored, and leadership is presented as the primary challenge facing administrators.

Human Relations Skills. The human relations skills unit is new. It deals with group behavior and dynamics, conflict management, and motivation of self and others. It provides the theoretical basis for the institute's insistence on affective as well as cognitive learning and for its stress on situational definitions of leadership and on the importance of gender socialization for administrative and leadership styles. It allows each participant to observe how she functions as a person and how her functioning is modified by the kinds of professional situations and institutional settings in which she finds herself at different times in her career.

Finance and Budgeting. The finance and budgeting unit — long the premier unit in the sense that most participants identify it as teaching the skills that they most need — focuses on accounting, budget procedures, and the strategy and politics of budgeting. Participant interest reflects a correct assessment of the primary importance of money and of information about its flow, acquisition, and allocation in the management of colleges and universities. The kinds of management information (statements and reports), ratio analysis, cash management, and long-range planning are examined in detail through lectures and case studies. Participants have the opportunity to analyze the financial statements of their own institutions, and issues related to finance are demystified.

Administrative Uses of the Computer. The unit on administrative uses of the computer provides basic vocabulary and concepts, financial and personal applications, and hands-on experience with diverse hardware and software. As with the finance and budgeting unit, the major thrust is to demystify a complex technical area so that participants can effectively question the persons in their home institutions who are charged with this function and so that they can supervise the activity when it falls in their area of responsibility. In the early years, the emphasis was on the use of mainframe-related technology. Now, it has shifted to the microcomputer and its applications for management, research, and teaching. Participant interest in this unit has grown dramatically, illustrating the recent surge of interest in this new technology.

Management and Leadership. The management and leadership unit focuses on basic concepts and skills in planning, organizing, staffing, and communicating. Legal issues and labor relations are also examined. The organizational structure of higher education is viewed in terms of functional areas, such as academic affairs, administrative services, public relations, development, personnel, and student services. Attention is given to the woman as manager and as leader, and expectations and perceptions conditioned by gender are explored.

The Diversity of American Higher Education

At its best and most ambitious, the Summer Institute seeks to encourage participants to think beyond themselves, their departments, and their institutions to examine the broad social issues with which American higher education must grapple. Higher education has assumed new and increasingly complex responsibilities since the end of World War II. By the year 2000, large numbers of students in America's colleges and universities will be minority. For many, English will be their second language. Women will continue to constitute more than half of the student population, and their numbers will continue to grow. How can the individual woman administrator prepare for this future? It is the philosophy of the Summer Institute that she can best prepare by learning firsthand what is happening in other parts of the country, in other countries, in other kinds of institutions to people, women and men, who are different from herself.

It is perhaps the finest achievement of the Summer Institute that it has been able to incorporate and accommodate the diversity that characterizes American higher education, both in the United States and in Canada. Over the last several years, minority enrollment has varied between 18 and 22 percent, and the group has included black women, Native American women, Asian Pacific women, and a growing number of Hispanic women, both from the mainland and from Puerto Rico. In the work situation, it is often easy to gloss over genuine differences of experience, background, and values. In sharp contrast, the Summer Institute provides the space, time, and incentive to meet and get to know other persons of different backgrounds and life-styles. Bridging differences is an important part of the Institute's work.

Institute participants are a varied group. The majority of women come from public institutions, they have the doctorate or the master's degree, they are in their thirties or forties, and they come from the faculty or are working in academic affairs. However, almost as many participants do not fit this profile. They have the bachelor's degree or no degree at all and many hard-won experiences; they are in their fifties and full of vision and energy; they come from church-related institutions with very carefully nurtured missions; they come from business affairs or student services. Most of these women come with preconceptions about administrators or faculty types and a lifetime of prejudices, some conscious, some not. Not everyone goes away friends, but most participants leave with a healthy respect for the many ways in which one can get a job done and for the many kinds of women who can do it. Networks depend on friendships, familiarity, and shared activities. The Summer Institute encourages these conditions.

The Network

The Summer Institute has committed a sizable proportion of its resources to the fostering of a network of peers, sponsors, and mentors who can provide one another with information, resources, useful contacts, and support. Developed through the interaction of participants among themselves and with faculty and staff during the course of the Summer Institute, the network is sustained and enlarged by means of a newsletter called the *Network,* a directory of institute alumnae and faculty, and reunions held throughout the country in conjunction with professional meetings and conferences.

The long-term goal of the network, as of the Summer Institute itself, is to develop a group of competent women administrators who have the skills and motivation to improve the employment situation of women on their campuses and in the nation at large. Teaching materials developed at the Summer Institute are also used by women in local and regional training programs. These local and regional activities have become the responsibility of the three HERS offices, which now refer to themselves collectively as the HERS Network. The HERS, New England office conducts an annual five-weekend administrative skills training program for women in that region. The HERS, Mid-America office has authored thirteen case studies of women administrators in such administrative areas as athletics and student services and in such roles as dean, administrative assistant, and trustee to allow for the study of administrative competencies and career issues. These cases can be used independently or in conjunction with HERS, Mid-America's campus-based in-service management and leadership program called "The Next Move." Finally, the HERS, West office conducts an annual five-day institute that provides professional development seminars and contacts with colleagues within its region and beyond. The regional networks interlock with the Summer Institute network and with the state programs conducted by the National Identification Program of the American Council on Education.

Conclusion

Each Summer Institute concludes with an elaborate individual exercise and participant panel entitled "Taking It Home." It is our deepest wish that each participant will take home what she has learned, together with a steadfast commitment to sharing her knowledge and energy with those who have not attended. We also hope that, to the best of her ability, she will use her individual creativity and institutional position to attack the organizational barriers and stubborn instances of personal prejudice that continue to slow the professional advancement of women and minorities.

References

Carnegie Commission. *Opportunities for Women in Higher Education.* New York: McGraw-Hill, 1973.

Tinsley, A. "Women in Administration." In *Proceedings of the Conference on Advancing Women in Higher Education Administration.* Madison: Office of Women, University of Wisconsin System, 1975.

Cynthia Secor, founding director of HERS, Mid-Atlantic, which for many years was based at the University of Pennsylvania, continues in this role with HERS, Mid-America, which is based at the University of Denver. She is cofounder and codirector of the Summer Institute for Women in Higher Education Administration.

Longitudinal evaluation of a series of five weekend seminars shows the impact of such a program on careers.

The Administrative Skills Program: What Have We Learned?

Jeanne J. Speizer

The Administrative Skills Program sponsored by HERS, New England at Wellesley College is designed to help women to advance in higher education administration. When it started in 1977, it used the year-long weekend format. To evaluate the effect that participation in the program would have on advancement, a longitudinal study, funded in part by a grant from the Fund for the Improvement of Post-Secondary Education, was built into the design. To assess the effects of a training program in career advancement, a comparison group had to be used. Thus, the HERS, New England study matched the first group of participants with a comparison group of nonparticipants. Job histories, career plans, and background information were collected from the members of both groups in 1978 and 1980. This chapter describes the Administrative Skills Program, the people who participated in it the first year, and the people in the comparison group; it reports on the findings of the follow-up study of the program's effectiveness in promoting advancement; and it relates the career histories and backgrounds of women administrators in the first group of participants to current theories about women in management.

The Program

The Administrative Skills Program is a seminar series designed for women administrators and faculty members who wish to prepare themselves

A. Tinsley, C. Secor, S. Kaplan, (Eds.). *Women in Higher Education Administration.*
New Directions for Higher Education, no. 45. San Francisco: Jossey-Bass, March 1984.

for further responsibility in educational management. The program consists of an integrated series of five weekend technical skills seminars—a total of ninety-eight hours spread over twelve days—which are held at Wellesley College over the course of an academic year. The first series was held in 1977–78. The program is ongoing and the sixth series was held in 1983–84.

The Administrative Skills Program has three goals: to provide participants with technical skills training that can upgrade job performance, promote advancement, or both; to establish a professional support network among women in the same geographic area; and to assist in the development of professional development tools for advancement. Six skills areas are covered: fiscal management, organizational behavior, management skills, information management, government and university relations, and professional development. Technical skills training sessions are designed and taught by faculty consultants with expertise in the area of concern, while the network-building activities and the professional development training are undertaken by HERS staff.

The curriculum is spread over several weekends to enable participants to test their skills learning in their own institutions, to work together with other participants, and to collect information from different divisions of their colleges or universities. This process ensures that participants will use the material that they learn in seminars on the job, that they will develop professional relationships with other participants, and that they will analyze the functional areas of their own institutions. When the women return to a subsequent session, they are able to discuss their findings and to examine the differences and variations among institutions and among various management organization systems.

Visibility is important to advancement, so several tactics have been built into the program to ensure that senior administrators are aware that women attending the program are interested in increased job responsibilities: Participants are encouraged to seek funding to attend the program to ensure the financial commitment of their institutions; a letter of recommendation from a supervisor is required for application to ensure that the home institution supports skills testing; and participants interview senior officials from all parts of the institution in order to obtain information about skills required and to understand the promotion paths and possibilities for higher-level positions.

Network building among participants is another key component of the program. It helps to overcome isolation, to improve contacts that can promote job advancement, and to provide support and information. Networks are developed among participants from the same institution and across institutions and state lines among participants with common interests and similar problems. Networks are considered useful in improving nominations for positions. Thus, participants are encouraged to share career goals and to seek other participants who might be able to help.

Evaluating the Program

To evaluate the effectiveness of the Administrative Skills Program in promoting advancement, participants in the first series of workshops completed a questionnaire about their backgrounds as part of the application procedure. These women constituted the experimental group. In spring 1978, a similar questionnaire was mailed to women administrators and faculty members who had requested information about the Administrative Skills Program but who had not applied to attend. These women constituted the comparison group. The questionnaire was completed and returned by 184 (70 percent) of those to whom it had been mailed. Two years later, in spring 1980, a three-page follow-up questionnaire was mailed to the 83 participants and to the 184 nonparticipants. Participants were also asked to complete a one-page questionnaire to determine how or whether they had used skills taught in the program on the job and to ascertain what other aspects of the program had proved useful for those who had attended. The follow-up questionnaire was remailed to nonrespondents. When all else failed, we telephoned nonrespondents to learn the present title and institution. Thus, follow-up information was obtained from 92 percent of the women who completed the original questionnaire.

The primary purpose of the follow-up questionnaire was to determine the impact of participation in the skills training program on job promotion. We defined advancement as a move upward that involves both a salary increase and increased control of people, resources, or both. However, as Moore and Sagaria (1981) point out, the similar but not identical titles that abound in postsecondary institutions create problems for classification. Mobility with advancement in responsibility is often unclear, because we lack a hierarchy of job titles. Thus, for purposes of the evaluation reported here, any job change is assumed to represent upward movement in title, responsibility, and salary unless the title classification or a comment by the respondent indicates that it is a demotion. Another outcome that we examined was change in career goals as manifested by further education or training or by a move to another field that might have better possibilities for advancement.

We collected personal, demographic, and career information on age, education, birth order, family status and history, career plans, job length, work history, area of administration, salary, and institution for present job. In the first stage of analysis we compared participants with nonparticipants to ascertain the similarities and differences between these two groups in background and such demographic variables as age, type of position, type of institution, family and fertility status, position in family of origin, and education. In the second stage of analysis, we compared the outcome variables of job change for the members of the two groups by three categories: same job, promotion, and other, which included returning to school, moving into another field of work, unemployment, retirement, and death. The aim of the comparisons was to assess the effect of participation in the program on promotion and job change. In the last stage of analysis, we looked at the entire population to determine how the background, demographic, and career information for the two groups was associated with administrative or faculty status in New England postsecondary institutions.

Findings

Of the 267 women administrators and faculty who completed the questionnaire in 1978, 74 (89 percent) members of the experimental group and 149 (81 percent) members of the comparison group returned the follow-up questionnaire in 1980 (Table 1). Current job status will be reported on a total of 246 women administrators and faculty: 79 (94 percent) in the experimental group and 167 (91 percent) in the comparison group. The twenty-one women who could not be located for the follow-up study and the twenty-three women who did not return the questionnaire but who were reached by telephone were compared with respondents in their respective cohorts on background and job information in 1978; there were no significant differences.

The 79 women in the experimental group and the 167 women in the comparison group for whom follow-up job status information was available were compared on 1978 background and job information to determine the similarity and differences between those in the two groups (Table 2). The groups were found to be similar in type of institution in which their members worked, in administrative area of work, and in salary, length of time in current position, and total number of years worked. However, there were twice as many faculty members in the experimental group (38 percent) as there were in the comparison group (18 percent).

Personal background information, most of which was collected in 1980, was compared for the two groups and again they were found to be similar (Table 3). Subjects ranged in age between twenty-five and sixty-two, and more than 65 percent of each group were less than forty-five years of age. The same percentage (29 percent) of each group had never been married. More women in the comparison group had no children. At least 50 percent of the women in both groups were the first born in their family. More women in the

Table 1. Responses from Experimental and Comparison Groups

	Total	Returned Questionnaire		Reached by Telephone	Total 1980		No Information 1980
Participants	83	74	(89%)	5	79	(94%)	4
Nonparticipants	184	149	(81%)	18	167	(91%)	17
Total	267	223	(84%)	23	246	(92%)	21

Table 2. Present Position, Experimental and Comparison Groups 1978

	Participants	Percent	Nonparticipants	Percent
	79		167	
Position[a]				
Faculty	30	38%	30	18%
Administrator	49	62	137	82
Administrative Area				
Student affairs	12	24	49	36
Academic affairs	20	41	33	24
Business affairs	13	27	45	33
Support staff	4	8	10	7
Type of Institution				
Public	33	42	62	37
Private	46	58	105	63
Research	22	28	56	34
Comprehensive	15	19	13	8
Liberal arts	30	38	73	45
Other	12	15	21	13
Salary[b]				
$15,000 or less	29	37	68	41
More than $15,000	49	63	96	59
Job Length				
One year	23	29	37	22
Two to five years	37	47	85	51
Six years or more	19	24	45	27
Total Years Worked[c]				
Ten years or less	23	31	54	36
Eleven to twenty years	34	46	65	44
Twenty-one years or more	17	23	30	20

[a] Chi square = 10.58; p = .002
[b] Salary data are missing for one participant and for three nonparticipants.
[c] This information was collected in 1980 for 74 participants and for 149 nonparticipants.

participant group had the doctorate, which may be related to the larger number of faculty members in that group.

Job status in 1980, two years after participants attended the first series of skills training seminars, was determined for members of the two groups in three categories: same job, promoted, or other. The other category included women who had returned to school, women who had left higher education for other fields, the unemployed, the retired, and the deceased (Table 4). Those in the other group were omitted from the analysis of factors related to promotion, since it was not clear whether they belonged in the same job group or in the promotion group. Promotion was defined as upgrading of a faculty position, a move from faculty to administration, or upgrading of an administrative posi-

Table 3. Personal Background Information

	Participants	Percent	Nonparticipants	Percent
	N = 79		N = 167	
Age				
Under 35	30	38%	56	34%
35–44	23	29	56	34
45–54	19	24	39	23
55 or older	7	9	16	9
Educational Level[a]				
Bachelor's	15	19	42	25
Master's	30	38	73	44
Doctorate	31	39	46	27
Birth Order[b]				
First	37	50	84	56
Second or later	37	50	65	44
Marital Status[b]				
Never married	21	29	41	29
Now married	34	47	76	54
Formerly married	17	24	25	17
Children[b]				
Yes	41	58	66	46
No	30	42	77	54

[a] Three participants and six nonparticipants had no degree.
[b] Information was collected in 1980, so data are presented for only 74 participants and 149 nonparticipants. Data for a few people are missing, since personal questions were described

tion. Twenty-four participants in the skills training program (30 percent) and thirty-four nonparticipants (20 percent) reported a promotion (Table 5).

Next, women who had not changed jobs in 1980 were compared with women who reported a promotion both within their respective cohorts and between groups, and job information collected in 1978 and personal back-

Table 4. Respondents Not Available for Promotion

	Participants	Percent	Nonparticipants	Percent	Total	Percent
	N = 79		N = 167		N = 246	
Student	2	3%	3	2%	5	2%
Working outside higher education	11	14	18	11	29	12
Unemployed	5	6	5	3	10	4
Retired or deceased	0	—	3	2	3	1
Totals	18	23%	29	17%	47	19%

Table 5. Respondents Promoted, 1978–1980

	Participants	Nonparticipants	Total
Promoted	24	34	58
Same position	37	104	141
	61	138	199[a]

[a]Chi square = 3.75; p = .056. Other group (47) and status unknown (4 participants and 17 nonparticipants) are not included.

ground information collected in 1978 and 1980 was used to determine what factors if any could explain the differences between these two groups (Table 6). The higher promotion rates for participants can be explained in part by the relative proportions of faculty and administrators, since there were approximately twice as many faculty members among participants (44 percent) as there were among nonparticipants (20 percent). Administrative promotions for participants occurred only in the academic and business affairs areas, while promotions for nonparticipating administrators were spread fairly evenly throughout the four administrative areas. Promotions were higher among participants from public institutions than they were for those from public institutions. For nonparticipants, there was essentially no difference. The largest percentage of promotions for participants was in the research and comprehensive universities. For the comparison group, type of institution made no difference. Salary, total number of years worked, and length of present job did not appear to be related to promotion for either group. Promotions were within institutions for more than 60 percent of those in each group who changed jobs. Thus, moves within their own institutions seemed to explain a large part of the job change possibilities available to members of both groups.

A number of personal background factors was considered as predictors of promotion in the period between 1978 and 1980 (Table 7). There were essentially no differences between participants and nonparticipants. In general, being younger (less than age forty-four), having the doctorate, being firstborn, not being married, and not having children all appeared to be associated with a greater likelihood of promotion.

Responses to career-planning questions showed few differences for the two groups. Women in both groups reported that both women and men provided advice and gave support to their actions and the issues that were important to them. Two thirds would consider alternative careers, but few reported plans for making career changes. In 1978, only about one third reported having received help from peers, mentors, supervisors, or influential others in obtaining their present positions, so at the start of the study few women were using contacts to get jobs.

As already noted, participants in the skills training program completed a separate questionnaire to ascertain the perceived effects of attendance. For

Table 6. Promotion Rates in 1980 Categorized by Job Information from 1978

	Participants			Nonparticipants		
	Same and Promoted	Number Promoted	Percent Promoted	Same and Promoted	Number Promoted	Percent Promoted
Position						
Faculty	27	14	52%[a]	27	9	33%
Administration	34	10	29	111	25	23
Administrative Area						
Student affairs	7	0	—	39	7	18
Academic affairs	16	6	38	28	5	18
Business affairs	9	4	44	34	9	26
Support staff	2	0	—	10	4	40
Type of Institution						
Public	25	8	32	56	12	21
Private	36	16	44[b]	82	22	26
Research	17	8	47[c]	45	12	27
Comprehensive	13	6	46[c]	11	3	27
Liberal arts	21	7	33	64	17	26
Other	10	3	30	14	1	7

[a] Faculty versus Administrators: chi square = 2.30; p = NS.
[b] Public versus Private: chi square = 0.5; p = NS.
[c] Research versus Liberal arts and other: chi square = 0.79; p = NS.

those in the promoted and other groups, 53 percent reported that participation in the program had been helpful for the changes that they had made. Forty-four percent of those who were still in the same job reported that they had added new skills and responsibilities to their work. More than half reported they had changed their career plans and goals as a result of the program.

Discussion

Two years is a short period of time in which to measure promotion. Nevertheless, administrators and faculty members who participated in the Administrative Skills Program were found to have experienced a faster promotion rate than those who did not. This finding must be considered within the parameters of self-selection, since we do not know why one group of women chose to attend and another asked for information but did not apply. Self-selection is a recurrent problem for the evaluation of special programs, since one rarely has the option to choose participants at random from the population as a whole. However, even within the constraints of self-selection, the Administrative Skills Program appeared to assist promotion in a remarkably short time. Thus, it can be recommended as a technique for hastening the advancement of women.

Table 7. Promotion Rates in 1980 Categorized by Personal Background Information from 1978

	Participants			Nonparticipants		
	Same and Promoted	Number Promoted	Percent Promoted	Same and Promoted	Number Promoted	Percent Promoted
Age						
Under 35	22	8	36%	46	15	33%
35–44	17	9	53	49	11	22
45–54	15	5	33	30	6	20
55 and above	7	2	29	13	2	15
Educational Level[a]						
Bachelor's	11	5	45	31	9	29
Master's	21	5	24	59	10	17
Doctoral	27	14	52	42	12	29
Birth Order[b]						
First	27	11	41	73	17	23
Second or later	31	11	35	56	15	27
Marital Status[b]						
Never married	16	10	62[c]	34	11	32[d]
Now married	29	9	31	71	15	21
Formerly married	12	2	17	19	4	21
Children[b]						
Yes	33	7	21	57	12	21
No	24	15	62[e]	67	19	28

[a]Three participants and six nonparticipants had no degree.
[b]Information was collected in 1980, so data are presented for only 58 participants and 129 nonparticipants. Data for a few people are missing, since personal questions were described as optional.
[c]Never married versus Now married and Formerly married: chi square = 4.94; p = .02.
[d]Never married versus Now married and Formerly married: chi square = 1.14; p = NS.
[e]Chi square = 8.44; p = .01.

It is not possible to explain why more faculty members than administrators who inquired about the program chose to attend. Many institutions developed a procedure to select participants who would receive institutional support to attend, and these procedures may have favored faculty members over administrators. Cutbacks have been more severe for faculty than for administrators, so it would not be surprising to find that many faculty members wished to attend a skills training program that might help them to move into administration. The academic track provides the greatest options for advancement to the top slots in an institution. If women faculty are using a skills training program to make a move into academic administration or if their institutions are identifying them to make such moves, we can be optimistic about these women's chances for moving into the higher echelons of management within the next ten years.

Moves within the institution were predominant for members of both groups. One would expect within-institution moves for women who received institutional support to attend, so the fact that internal moves were predominant for both groups indicates that the options for within-institution moves now outnumber the options for interinstitutional moves. This finding is consistent with those of most current studies of how administrators obtained their present jobs. Thus, special projects that provide visibility and signal that women are interested in moving upwards can be recommended. Such special programs may increase the number of women who are able to advance.

Taken together, the women administrators and faculty members in the two groups provide a profile of the background and career histories of women administrators currently working in postsecondary institutions. The presence of so many firstborn children in the ranks of managers suggest that firstborn women experience a different socialization from women who are born into families with boys or who are not the first born. Yet, these women managers are still to be found in the lower ranks. If socialization explains the success or failure of women, then the socialization that encourages a high proportion of firstborn women to pursue a managerial career should help them to reach the top of the pyramid. That it does not means that other factors must explain why firstborn women strive in great numbers to join the managerial ranks, and then are not able to progress in equal proportion with their male colleagues.

The presence of children also appears to have an effect on promotion, since two thirds of the participants who were promoted did not have children. The Administrative Skills Program was held on weekends, so it would not be surprising to find that women with children chose not to attend. However, more participants than nonparticipants had children. Nearly three fourths of the participants who stayed in their present jobs had children. Single parenting may be a factor, since few who were formerly married were promoted. As the members of each group tended to be young — half were under age forty — it would not be surprising to find that marriage and having children are two important factors that women were considering when planning for advancement. Two years is too little time in which to assess the effects of marriage and having a family on promotion rates for women.

The study does not tell us what specific aspects of the skills training program were most useful for promotion. However, in addition to the skills learned, the visibility that accrued from the selection process, letters of support, interviews, requests for institutional funding, and on-the-job testing of learned skills were all reported to have been important by those who advanced. The regional network contacts that participants made were also reported to have been important for career advancement and in setting career goals. Women had a chance to overcome the isolation of their positions and institutions by interacting with program faculty and other participants and by learning about organizational structures and job possibilities that they had not previously envisioned. The effects of network contacts are not immediately visible, but as Brown (1981, p. 59) states, "there is no doubt that [networks] can be of some use, especially in a job market where, as the U.S. Bureau of Labor Statistics shows, almost half—48 percent—of all jobs come through personal contacts." Capek (1982) reports that networks for women administrators appear to be working. If she is correct, it can be predicted that participants will find that the network formed by working together over the course of a year in the skills training program will be an important ingredient in their advancement.

Postsecondary institutions need more women administrators to match the rising number of women in the student population. Left to their own devices, higher education institutions appear to add women students with ease and to increase the number of women managers with difficulty. The Administrative Skills Program was designed to accelerate the advancement of women. The evidence presented in this chapter indicates that the Administrative Skills Program strategy appears to work.

References

Brown, L. K. *The Woman Manager in the United States: A Research Analysis and Bibliography.* Washington, D.C.: Business and Professional Women's Foundation, 1981.

Capek, M. E. *Higher Education Administrators in New Jersey: A Preliminary Report on Research Findings.* Princeton, N.J.: Princeton University, in cooperation with American Council on Education, 1982.

Moore, K. M., and Sagaria, M. A. "Women Administrators and Mobility: The Second Struggle." *Journal of the National Association of Women Deans, Administrators, and Counselors,* 1981, *44,* 21–28.

Jeanne J. Speizer designed and directed the Administrative Skills Program for HERS, New England, at Wellesley College from 1977 to 1982.

In the past eight years, the number of women college and university presidents in the United States has risen from 154 to 253, a gain of 99 and an increase of 65 percent. The American Council on Education's National Identification Program has played a significant role in this achievement.

Toward a New Era of Leadership: The National Identification Program

Donna Shavlik
Judy Touchton

Until recent years, the assumption that leaders are drawn from the ranks of men was rarely questioned. Higher education was no exception. Less than a decade ago, men held 95 percent of all college and university presidencies. Of the women presidents, two thirds were members of religious orders, and most of the others headed colleges primarily for women.

As the second women's movement of this century began to be felt in the early 1970s, some leaders in higher education become more conscious of the role of women and of their virtual absence from leadership circles. In 1972, the American Council on Education (ACE) became the first higher education association to hold a national conference focused on women's issues. At that time, the ACE board of directors decided to establish an Office of Women in Higher Education (OWHE) and a Commission on Women in Higher Education to advice it. Several factors contributed to this decision: ACE had a new president; influential women were members of the board, men and women on the ACE staff were committed to these ideas, and senior women from ACE member institutions had offered their advice and involvement. The Office of Women and the commission were formed in spring 1973, marking the third

A. Tinsley, C. Secor, S. Kaplan, (Eds.). *Women in Higher Education Administration.*
New Directions for Higher Education, no. 45. San Francisco: Jossey-Bass, March 1984.

time in its history that ACE had created within its own organization a special group to address women's concerns. In 1920, ACE had established a standing committee on the training of women for public service, which lasted for a short time. In 1953, it created a commission on the education of women, which remained in existence for eight years. The work of that commission was substantial and significant, as it dealt with a number of critical issues for women that emerged in the postwar era (Astin, 1976).

Between 1973 and 1975, commission members and OWHE staff began to document the relative and sometimes total absence of women from top levels of administration in all educational systems and all sectors—public and private, two-year and four-year, large institution and small. Since women then accounted for almost half of the students and for a quarter of the faculty in higher education, their mere 5 percent share of the presidencies stood out in sharp contrast. It was impossible not to recognize the inequity and the loss of talent.

The absence of women from positions of prominence did not mean that there were no women leaders in higher education, nor did it mean that higher education had failed to develop and use women leaders. The problem seemed to have been created by the relative invisibility of women as major leaders within and beyond their own campuses and communities. When women were called upon to address this problem, they realized that they knew numerous other women across the country who held key positions and who were quite influential—often far more influential than their titles would lead one to believe. Some men also knew women in such positions. Nevertheless, their relative lack of visibility, with some other crucial factors—perceptual bias, sex-role stereotyping, institutional sexism—accounted for much of the problem.

Increased awareness led ACE staff and commission members to formulate a response. As the major coordinating association for higher education, ACE seemed to be the most appropriate organization to address the issue created by the paucity of women in leadership roles. ACE constituents include colleges and universities, state and national education associations, other specialized institutions, and groups concerned with higher education. Moreover, most representatives of these organizations to ACE are chief executive officers. Thus, any explorations of equity and access that the organization undertook would begin at the top.

Deliberations by staff, commissioners, and numerous advisers led in January 1977 to the creation of the National Identification Program for the Advancement of Women in Higher Education Administration, which is often referred to as ACE/NIP. The program was funded by a substantial grant from the Carnegie Corporation of New York and by institutional support from ACE. The major intent of ACE/NIP is to expand the pool of persons qualified for leadership roles in our nation's colleges and universities so that all women—black, Hispanic, Asian Pacific, Asian American, Native American, and white—can have opportunities for advancement and so that higher education can benefit from the richness of their participation.

Conceptualizing the NIP

Because of ACE's involvement with senior administrators, the Office of Women in Higher Education and the Commission on Women in Higher Education decided to focus on increasing the number of women in higher education administration, with special emphasis on presidencies, vice-presidencies, and deanships. The first step in establishing the program was to examine the systemic barriers to women's advancement. These included a widespread belief within the higher education community that not many women were really qualified to assume major responsibilities within institutions, a lack of interest or an unconscious disinterest in recognizing and promoting women leaders, and a habitual inability to recruit and support women leaders. The natural tendency of executive management to select and promote people like themselves (Kanter, 1977), the isolation of women administrators, and the tendency of women to compare themselves with an ideal of leadership (men compare themselves with other men) constitute other barriers. Finally, the absence of a comprehensive set of networks enabling new and different people to enter the leadership ranks, failure to understand that institutions could be greatly improved by adding women and minorities to the leadership pool, failure to recognize that most training for management and leadership roles occurs on the job and women should be hired for their potential, just as men are, and the problems created for minority women by double discrimination compound the problem.

The National Identification Program addressed these barriers through goals designed to identify talented women, to work to enhance their visibility as leaders, and to increase their opportunities for advancement; to create, sustain, and enrich networks of women and men, minority and majority, who were committed to women's leadership and who could identify, recommend, and sponsor women; to improve higher education by increasing the pool of potential exemplary leaders; to target barriers to women's advancement and develop programs and other strategies with which to address them; and to work for the advancement of all women.

As the program developed, it became apparent that building a series of interdependent and interlocking networks would be the best way of addressing existing personal and systemic barriers. In effect, these strategies created a new voluntary association designed to focus attention on the advancement of women in higher education administration under the aegis of the ACE.

The problem was that many more women in higher education were qualified for leadership roles than were represented in the leadership ranks. The operating philosophy of the NIP was based on the beliefs that women are fully as competent and well prepared as men, that higher education deserves the benefit of their leadership as much as they deserve the chance to lead, and that women are willing to struggle with the existing system of higher education to make the changes needed for higher education to foster and accept women as leaders. Initially, participants in the NIP were defined as administrative women — those currently serving as department chair, assistant or associate dean, dean, or vice-president — who were ready for advancement to a deanship, vice-presidency, or presidency.

Establishing and Defining the NIP: Structure, People, Funding

Structure: A Framework, Not a Blueprint. The architects of the NIP believed that the primary goal of the program — to increase the number of competent women in policy-making positions in higher education administration — could be accomplished most effectively by carefully constructed state-based programs complemented by other activities that were national in scope. The structure and design of the program reflected this approach.

Originally, the general plan included selection of state coordinators who held high-level administrative posts; appointment of state planning committees composed of representatives of all higher education systems within each state; formation of state panels of men and women who influence and shape public policy; advice from coordinators, planning committee members, and panelists on ways of improving efforts to identify and advance competent women; appointment of a national panel of prominent educators to enhance the system of state networks; and the holding of several ACE national forums to promote acquaintanceship and exchange of ideas among women leaders and national panelists.

All these components of the original plan are still in place and still considered essential. New components have been added as needs have emerged and as new ideas and strategies have been developed. These new components include Women Executive Seminars, which give groups of women administrators with similar position titles an opportunity to come together to discuss common issues and concerns; Focus on Minority Women's Advancement (FMWA), a program designed to concentrate attention and energy on issues of particular concern to the advancement of minority women — black, Hispanic, Asian Pacific, Asian American, and Native American — and to ensure that such women are thoroughly involved in all aspects of the NIP; appointment of distinguished women administrators in or near retirement as NIP senior associates to share their wisdom and expertise with other women in the program; ACE/NIP regional forums, which give key persons in the NIP an opportunity to meet in their respective geographical regions to discuss educational issues of regional concern, to renew acquaintances, and to extend the growing networks within each state; involvement of women trustees in ongoing NIP activities and special meetings that allow women trustees to discuss their own particular issues; appointment of association liaisons to create formal links with key national education associations and to further the commitment of these associations to women's advancement; and encouraging and making nominations and recommendations of women well known to the program for presidencies, vice-presidencies, and deanships.

With the exception of the Women Executive Seminars and the ACE/ NIP regional forums, all these components are ongoing aspects of the NIP. Time, energy, and funding permitting, all past and present programs could be doubled, and the needs of women and the higher education community would still not be met.

People: The Real Source of Change. The NIP now involves more than 6,000 women and men administrators who volunteer their time and energy in ways that help the program to succeed. Certain of these people play special roles in the NIP: state coordinators, state planning committee members, state and national panelists, FMWA consultants, senior associates, association liaisons, selected women trustees, participants in national forums, and OWHE staff.

State Coordinators. State coordinators are the backbone of the NIP. Selected for their high-level positions, leadership ability, and commitment to the advancement of women, coordinators play a critical role in shaping and implementing the goals of the NIP in each state. The fifty-three current coordinators, who represent the fifty states plus New York City, the District of Columbia, and Puerto Rico, collectively hold a variety of positions in academic affairs, student affairs, administrative affairs, and external affairs. Four of the current coordinators are minority women.

Coordinators play a vital role in articulating the goals of the NIP, in coordinating the efforts of planning committees, in generating resources to support the program, and in serving as chief contact person for the state program. Individual coordinators vary considerably in their leadership styles, and they handle their work with planning committees in a variety of ways. In the early days of the NIP, state coordinators typically worked closely with OWHE staff to explore and resolve questions of direction, personnel, organization, and financing and to plan programs and other strategies. As they gained experience and confidence and as the state programs themselves matured, most coordinators became able to work with OWHE staff at a different level. Initially, staff traveled frequently to the states to attend planning committee meetings and state programs. Now, consultation occurs chiefly by telephone, and most communication is handled by mail. Staff visit the states only for statewide programs and as resources permit.

State Planning Committee Members. State planning committees are typically composed of ten to fifteen women administrators representing all systems of higher education in the state. More than 600 women currently serve on these committees, and at least 200 others have served in the past. Planning committees work with the state coordinators, the OWHE, and the state panelists to develop effective strategies for identifying and promoting the advancement of women within the state. Statewide conferences are part of every state program and inter- and intrastate conferences are becoming frequent. Most states have found it useful to restrict some conferences to women only and to hold other conferences that include men, since each type serves different networking needs. Increasingly, however, states are employing strategies other than conferences and seminars to promote women's advancement. These new strategies include visiting individual panelists to engage them to support women leaders, holding joint meetings with influential higher education groups in the state, nominating and recommending women for positions and special opportunities, developing campus-based networks to promote women's leadership, and strengthening links with other influential women's networks in the state.

State and National Panelists. State and national panelists are leaders in higher education or in positions to influence higher education who accept the invitation of ACE to join its national network of influential women and men who are interested in the identification and advancement of highly competent women. Panelists include college and university presidents, trustees, association heads, public officials, and civic leaders who have a special interest in higher education. Panelists play a variety of roles in the NIP, according to their preferences and styles. For many, simply allowing their names to be identified with the program makes a valuable contribution. Other roles include meeting with individual women administrators identified by the program at professional conferences or on their own campuses; nominating or recommending women administrators for professional positions, for membership on boards, councils, committees, or as speakers or presenters at programs; attending state or national forums or other programs sponsored by the NIP; and providing resources to the program. Approximately 240 people currently serve on the national panel, and about 750 serve on state panels across the nation.

FMWA Consultants. To accomplish the goals of the Focus on Minority Women's Advancement, the OWHE developed regional networks of persons who concentrate on the advancement of minority women. National and regional consultants representing black, Hispanic, Asian Pacific, Asian American and Native American women work with the OWHE as consultants to FMWA. Their roles include assisting in the identification of minority women, initiating contact with both emerging and well-established minority women's networks, and suggesting activities that ACE can organize or encourage others to organize that will address the needs of minority women in higher education and improve their status. Thirteen women currently serve as consultants. Five work with specific geographical regions, and eight work generally with the office on specific issues.

Senior Associates. Senior associates are distinguished women executives at or near the point of retirement who represent ACE and the OWHE in state and national NIP activities. Five senior associates — four former college presidents (one minority) and the former director of the OWHE — now serve in this capacity. By traveling, speaking, and consulting for the NIP and by serving as mentors and role models to women across the country, the senior associates extend OWHE's capacity to seek positive institutional change. An overriding principle of the NIP is to encourage each person — state leader, national leader, or woman administrator identified by the program — to assume individual responsibility for the advancement of women in leadership roles in higher education. Senior associates are uniquely valuable in this process, since they attend state programs and participate in working sessions with panelists to whom they can relate as peers. They are doubly appreciated by women administrators who live in states where there are as yet no women presidents to serve as models.

Association Liaisons. The role of association liaison was conceived of as a means of enhancing efforts already under way by the major higher education associations to promote the advancement of talented women administrators. The major goals of this role are to assist women and panelists in the associations who have been active in the NIP to use occasions and meetings organized by the associations to renew acquaintances and strengthen networking, to continue the process of identifying and promoting outstanding women leaders, and to advise on activities that could further enhance the role of women in institutions represented by these associations. Persons invited to serve in this capacity are senior women who have been involved in the NIP and who are already influential within their respective associations. The liaisons work with ACE and OWHE staff to plan social events or seminars at the annual meetings of their associations. They also help to identify other ways of promoting women's advancement under association auspices. Currently, there are eight association liaisons.

Participants in National Forums. The idea of holding ACE national forums was conceived of in the first year of the National Identification Program as a means of connecting talented senior women administrators with one another and with leaders in higher education. Of the twenty women who attended the first forum in fall 1977, seven were appointed to presidencies within the next few years. Since 1977, twenty-nine national forums involving almost 600 women and 200 national panelists have been held. At last count, approximately one third of the women who had attended forums had changed positions, and twenty-nine had become college or university presidents. Many other women have reported expansion of their role and influence within the same job or appointments to key commissions or boards.

In planning the forums, it was anticipated that contacts would represent an important step in personalizing the identification process and that contacts made at forums would continue in other modes. These expectations have been realized. Participants and panelists alike have reported numerous contacts following the forums, many of which resulted in nominations, recommendations, or consultations regarding positions or membership on advisory boards, councils, and committees. For women, the forums have fostered professional activity, increased levels of professional involvement, and promoted visibility. For men, the forums have heightened their awareness of the number of talented women in higher education and made them more receptive to leadership from women.

Funding. NIP's funding has come from the ACE, the Carnegie Corporation of New York, several small grants, and in-kind contributions by countless individuals and institutions committed to and involved with the program.

The Carnegie Corporation awarded three successive grants to the ACE in support of the National Identification Program in the seven years between 1977 and 1983. Several smaller grants from other private and some public sources made it possible to initiate particular projects within the NIP. These sources include the Donner Foundation, the Exxon Education Foundation, the Ford Foundation, the Fund for the Improvement of Post-Secondary Education, the Johnson Foundation, the National Institute of Education, the Phillips Foundation, and the Women's Educational Equity Act.

Strategies

Influencing the way in which people think and the choices that they make regarding women's leadership ability and potential is a major focus of all strategies. For example, it becomes hard to believe that there are few outstanding women leaders when one finds oneself in a room full of them. Many strategies used by the NIP were designed specifically to feature emerging women leaders in management, speaking, and teaching roles so that established leaders could see them in action. Although classification of NIP strategies is difficult, four categories can be singled out for attention here: convening strategies, consultative strategies, systemic strategies, and personal strategies.

Convening Strategies. Many of the strategies most often used by the NIP simply involve bringing people together who need to meet and who have no formal mechanism for doing so. From informal receptions to highly organized seminars and conferences, from women-only meetings to meetings attended by few women and many men, from single-issue conferences to multiple program conferences, from initiating new conferences to bringing women into established conferences, states have used every possible kind of meeting, workshop, seminar, roundtable, symposium, forum, and conference.

The success of these events, whether they take place at the state or the national level, depends on setting a tone of high expectation, mutual learning, and continuing support. For example, one of the current women presidents is certain that she is president now because the right people heard her give an outstanding speech at an early NIP statewide conference. The content was excellent, many colleagues reported, but the necessary additional ingredient was the presence that she brought to the role. People were able to see her as a president. In another example of somewhat different scope, a male panelist who was the first man to arrive at a NIP meeting where many women were already present had a sudden realization of what it feels like to be in the minority. Countless examples of experiences that have permanently altered careers and attitudes can be presented.

Consultative Strategies. Early in the development of the NIP, a proposal to publish a directory of top-level women administrators was rejected in favor of systematic and purposeful efforts to build a person-to-person system of contacts that could serve to expand the network of leaders in higher education. Individual and group consultation strategies have been critical to these efforts. Conferences, seminars, and meetings of various kinds consistently include activities that encourage and legitimize the giving and receiving of personal assistance. Frequently, they include opportunities to discuss the interview process, to conduct practice interview sessions, and to talk about career plans. The importance of these consultations cannot be underestimated. Established leaders provide willing counsel and information to women whom they meet through the program. These conversations, whether they occur in person or by telephone, constitute a major outcome of NIP's state and national gatherings. As a direct result, women have increased their levels of confidence, learned new ways of presenting their strengths in person and on paper, and discovered new heights to which they can aspire. At the same time, established leaders have met many highly talented women and been impressed by their knowledge and skills.

Systemic Strategies. Although many people have become more aware in recent years of personal attitudes and behaviors that discriminate against women, few realize the ways in which institutions also inadvertently perpetuate sex discrimination. For example, institutional employment policies often build in discriminatory mechanisms that affect recruitment practices, promotion and tenure, salary and benefit packages, and maternity and paternity leave, to name only a few. Thus, effecting change in relevant system policies, practices, and procedures constitutes a major challenge for the NIP.

Two critical areas that the NIP addresses are the search and selection processes for administrative staff in general and for chief executive officers in particular. In addressing the search process, the NIP consistently emphasizes two points: First, even before initiating a search, search committees and hiring authorities must openly address and come to terms with the issue of women in leadership roles so that unconscious or unexpressed bias against the hiring of women will not subvert the process. Second, the persons responsible for the search must be willing to stop the search process at any point if it becomes clear that the process is not yielding a candidate pool containing qualified women and minority candidates.

NIP planning committees meet with various organizations within state structures of education — governing boards, coordinating boards, state education departments, and state organizations of colleges and universities — to address the systematic ways in which women are prevented from participating in the activities that lead to recognition of their talents and eventually to promotion. In various settings, planning committees have presented programs on the search process and how it can be improved, presented data on the status of women in the state, and offered the NIP as a resource that can be used to develop programs and seek talented women to serve in leadership roles. Occasionally, such presentations have caused changes in hiring practices and procedures.

The Washington office of the NIP works directly with search committees, presidents, and board members to complement the efforts of national and state NIP programs to improve the search process and to expand the pool of persons who can be considered for senior administrative positions. Most of this work comes in response to requests for nominations, for information about potential women candidates, and for advice and counsel regarding the search process. The experience of the OWHE indicates that the number of institutions that are genuinely seeking talented women candidates has increased substantially over the past few years, as has the number of women appointed to senior administrative posts.

Institutional barriers to women's advancement have also been discussed at national and regional forums, and some changes have resulted from the interventions of individuals whose attitudes have been altered by these discussions. In recent years, one of the issues most often raised has been the selection of chief executive officers. There is concern that presidential candidates whose spouses are willing to assume a major volunteer role are at an advantage in the search process, since boards of trustees have traditionally valued the contributions of the presidential couple and expected both members to provide primary service to the institution. After much discussion, the ACE board of directors passed a resolution in October 1983 recommending that college and university governing boards choose presidents "solely on the basis of their ability to carry out the responsibilities of the office" and stating that "race, sex, ethnicity, age, physical disability, or marital status should not be used to prevent a person from being selected as a chief executive officer" (American Council on Education, 1983). The resolution emphasized the importance of defining and clearly articulating the social expectations of chief executive officers and of providing for appropriate recognition and resources. Besides supporting the important and significant role of the professional volunteer spouse, such an approach to presidential selection legitimizes the new roles increasingly seen in the life-styles of many presidential candidates, notably married and single women, single men, and married men whose wives prefer a limited role.

Personal Strategies. All the ideas, contacts, support, and opportunities afforded by the NIP are useless unless they are incorporated by each individual. Personal integration is the key. Each person makes a special contribution and gains in direct proportion to that contribution. The program works best for individuals who learn from it, who work with the ideas that it presents, who examine their perspectives anew, and who take initiative for themselves and others. This may seem obvious, but the strength of it is profound.

Conclusion

Of the many insights that have emerged from the NIP, two seem especially significant: Women in the NIP gain a sense of empowerment and worth by having access to the leadership of higher education and to those who influence leaders, and men in the NIP gain new respect for the quality of women's leadership and an awareness that there are more women leaders than they ever imagined.

Encouraging and fostering women's leadership through getting acquainted, nominating, recommending, and supporting is invaluable. It still seems true that women play these roles for each other more effectively than men do for women (Capek, 1982). However, surveys of panelists conducted by the OWHE and panelists' personal anecdotes indicate that men are becoming increasingly involved in the process of promoting women.

Getting women administrators to meet with one another has had some valuable results: a growing sense of respect for one another, a genuine belief in the overall competence and value of women, and an overall sense of female bonding. These results have fostered participants' commitment to the larger goals of the program even when specific activities do not work perfectly. At the first national forum the women were self-conscious, as were the established leaders and NIP staff. This self-consciousness has now grown into confidence and pride — in themselves and in the program.

Maintaining the belief that change is possible and sustaining efforts to foster change can be wearing, if not exhausting. Constantly communicating the spirit, the progress, and the goals of the NIP remain critical functions for the national office and all NIP's programs. Any program that depends on volunteers who have conflicting commitments and insufficient time needs a core staff who constantly put the program first. Nurturing and tending the network, encouraging and supporting the volunteers remain essential and necessary roles of the national office staff.

In the eight years since the NIP began, the number of women presidents in the United States has risen from 154 to 253 (Shavlik and Touchton, 1984), an increase of 65 percent. This increase, which is unprecedented in our nation's history, is the result of many efforts in the past few years to change and improve the status of women. With its focus on moving women into major leadership roles in higher education, the NIP has been one of these efforts. Twenty-nine of the ninety-nine women presidents appointed since 1977 have attended ACE national forums, and others have been involved in numerous aspects of the program. The program continues to give recognition and visibility to these competent women leaders and to enhance their already distinguished careers.

Minority women are also being appointed to college presidencies in increasing numbers, although these numbers as yet remain small. In 1975, there were fewer than five minority women presidents, and most of them headed community colleges. Today, seventeen chief executive officers are minority women — fourteen are black, one is Hispanic, one is Asian American, and one is Native American — and four of the black women head four-year institutions. As in the case of their majority counterparts, minority women represent a large pool of underutilized talent. Many minority women identified through the NIP should already be in major leadership roles.

Despite these gains, some problems remain. Differential salaries for administrators and faculty members are still very prominent in the educational environment. In spite of the growing number of women presidents, only 9 percent of all colleges and universities are currently headed by women, and only 1 percent are headed by minority women. Although the national figures reflect an overall increase, the numbers of senior administrative women have actually declined in some states. Women are still absent from many influential programs and decision-making groups or so underrepresented that their contribution is minimized. Higher education can ill afford such a loss of talent.

Where do we go from here? When women constitute half of the leadership in higher education, when minority women constitute an integral part of that leadership, and when the impact of women's involvement results in new and effective directions in higher education, the services of the National Identification Program and related action programs will no longer be necessary. Until that time, special efforts that make women's advancement their primary focus are imperative. Women deserve to be leaders, and our society has long needed the kind of leadership that they can provide.

References

American Council on Education (ACE). Resolution on Selection of Chief Executive Officers of Colleges and Universities. Passed by the ACE Board of Directors, Toronto, Ontario, Canada, October 12, 1983.

Astin, H. S. (Ed.). *Some Action of Her Own.* Lexington, Mass.: Heath, 1976.

Capek, M. E. *Higher Education Administrators in New Jersey: A Preliminary Report on Research Findings.* Princeton, N.J.: Princeton University, in cooperation with the American Council on Education, 1982.

Kanter, R. M. *Men and Women of the Corporation.* New York: Basic Books, 1977.

Shavlik, D., and Touchton, J. *Women Chief Executive Officers in Colleges and Universities, Table VIII.* Washington, D.C.: Office of Women in Higher Education, American Council on Education, 1984.

Donna Shavlik is director of the Office of Women in Higher Education of the American Council on Education (ACE). She directs the National Identification Program for the Advancement of Women in Higher Education Administration (ACE/NIP).

Judy Touchton is associate director of the Office of Women in Higher Education of the American Coucil on Education. She shares responsibility for directing the National Identification Program for the Advancement of Women in Higher Education Administration.

Networks for minority women provide information, support, and an arena where minority issues can take priority on the agenda.

Lifting as We Climb: Networks for Minority Women

Margaret B. Wilkerson

Long before networking became popular as a means of achieving personal advancement, it was a means of survival for blacks and other minorities. Now defined in the professional literature as "collectivizing one's contacts" for a particular end (Metha, 1979, p. 31), it was formerly known simply as "staying in touch" among those whose lives often depended on knowing what places to avoid when moving or traveling across the country.

One never knew what dangers or insults would be encountered along the way. The Darden sisters (Darden and Darden, 1978, p. 246) have described their summer trips in the South as children: "Racist policies loomed like unidentified monsters in our childish imaginations and in reality. After the New Jersey Turnpike ended, we would have to be on the alert for the unexpected. So, as we approached that last Howard Johnson's before Delaware, our father would make his inevitable announcement that we had to get out, stretch our legs, and go to the bathroom, whether we wanted to or not. This was a ritualized part of every trip, for, although there would be many restaurants along the route, this was the last one that didn't offer segregated facilities. From this point on, we pulled out our trusty shoe box lunches. Any discomfort during these yearly travels was balanced by a sense of adventure, for, after we finished our shoe box lunches, we would have to keep our eyes peeled for black-owned establishments, which usually took us off the main route. If we needed a place to sleep before reaching our destination, we would have to ask random

A. Tinsley, C. Secor, S. Kaplan, (Eds.). *Women in Higher Education Administration.*
New Directions for Higher Education, no. 45. San Francisco: Jossey-Bass, March 1984.

fellow blacks where accommodations could be found. Often, total strangers would come to our rescue, offering lodging and feeding us as well. We made many new friends this way, as hospitality and solidarity were produced by tight segregation. How different traveling in the South is today! But, in spite of all the really remarkable changes, we have continued the habit of stopping with our old friends as we travel."

When I was a child driving with my family from Los Angeles to Oklahoma City, I quickly learned what it meant to be without a network. Racial discrimination forced us out of public restaurants and hotels in Arizona and New Mexico, and the scarcity of facilities along Route 66 as we drove across the desert meant spending a couple of days and nights in states in which contacts were extremely limited. Sometimes, we drove all night to cover the distance without stopping, or we parked off the road for a couple of hours to get a little sleep.

For Mexican Americans, Chicanos, Puerto Ricans, and other Hispanic peoples, the situation was similar. The few dollars available went into the gas tank, while friends and relatives along the way gladly provided a meal or a bed. Those who traveled by train, especially blacks, found a network among the porters — every family either had a family member or a friend or relative who worked as a porter — who would see to it that young children traveling alone were safely delivered to their destination or who knew what hotels and restaurants were open to minorities in any city along the route. Although these networks served the basic needs of food and shelter, they carried news as well: news about jobs and about the social and economic climate for minorities in any city or region.

Women of color have a long tradition of activist networks. The Underground Railroad is perhaps the best known. Women like Harriet Tubman, who was known as "the general," led numerous black slaves to freedom through a complicated arrangement of way stations in risky ventures undertaken in collaboration with both whites and blacks. The first national conference for colored women was held in Boston in 1895. An early formal network of black women, this meeting resulted in the formation of a national coalition whose agenda included such issues as job prospects and training, education, political equality, temperance, and racism. In the 1960s, the women supporters of the Student Nonviolent Coordinating Committee who organized networks to monitor the treatment of jailed demonstrators and who identified safe havens for endangered students helped to empower a civil rights movement that changed the face of the country. Those networks were organized to attack huge social problems: slavery, lynching, denial of civil rights and educational opportunity, and other major issues. Traditionally, minority women have organized to take on the largest of questions. Despite the perception that they were the least powerful of all, they dared to speak out and to organize campaigns against racism and sexism with the barest of resources and sometimes with minimal support from white women.

Today's questions are just as large, partly as a result of their persistence.

How do we create opportunity for people of color and others who find themselves locked in a cycle of poverty and alienation? How do we build the will and the interest to tackle this question in those who have resources? How do we affirm ethnic identity and foster communication in a world confused by diversity? How can we use the power and influence of educational institutions, government, and business to improve the quality of human life for everyone? Important as these questions are, attempts to answer them must now also face the strong drive for personal advancement and individual mobility as discussion of networking comes to center on the immediate and the readily attainable. As minority women contemplate the development and perpetuation of networks in the 1980s, they must take their legacy of activism into account and ask, Networks for what? Are personal advancement and social mobility the only ends that we seek? Do we seek more money? Greater influence? To what end?

Lift as We Climb was the answer given a century ago as newly freed blacks struggled to loose the bonds of slavery and ignorance. The commitment of the historically black colleges to admit students whom other institutions might reject and to open the world of learning to these students was embodied in that phrase. It is still pertinent to women of color in the 1980s, for it acknowledges their need and desire for personal advancement while connecting them with a collective effort to improve the quality of life for many. It places individual ambition in context and allows it to replenish and recreate itself through those who follow. This maxim asks us to return to the community some of the nurturing and support that allowed us to succeed. This kind of commitment has given a poignant ring to the word *education* among minority peoples and suggested an obligation to open the way for others by sharing knowledge and influence in a way that will liberate, not enslave. Lift as we climb became the guiding principle for many organizing efforts in the early twentieth century, as those blessed with education worked to bring others along to fill new places.

The needs of the 1980s might seem counter to this concept. Much of the current literature on networking emphasizes its personal nature and approaches the idea largely in terms of a single aspect—personal ambition. While personal ambition is a necessary ingredient of getting ahead and capitalizing on one's opportunities, it achieves success only for one individual, and it may work to the detriment of others who have contributed to that individual's success. Personal ambition takes but seldom gives, and it often exaggerates the individual's sense of accomplishment. Of course, even success as a token can be a heady experience. A token is compared, almost always favorably, to other minorities, mostly out of ignorance and self-adulation. She has high visibility, a necessary requirement of token status. She speaks with authority—at least on the issues that are supposed to relate to people of color. And, she may begin to fear that others will threaten her position. She may also be quite vulnerable if she is alienated from a power base. Lift as we climb may sound old-fashioned, but if we do not heed it the gains of token status are likely to be short-lived.

What are the networking needs of minority women in this decade? The primary need is empowerment — control over policy that affects one's life — and the opportunity to move an agenda that promotes quality and excellence unhampered by inequity and discrimination. Specific needs differ with the individual situation. For example, minority women students need financial, academic, and psychological support to pursue an education and a career. Many face financial problems, and they are often discouraged by faculty who place little faith in their intellectual capabilities. Minority women professionals need opportunities to demonstrate their capabilities and recognition of their achievements through promotion or assignment to jobs with greater responsibility. Too many college administrators overlook minority women because, they say, they "are doing such a good job where they are," or because their "difference" is unfamiliar and perhaps threatening to collegiate customs, or because they are in dead-end jobs. Networks for minority women need enlightened administrators who can share information on career development and who recognize and reward talent and ability.

Collective sharing among minority women is the beginning of empowerment, as knowledge is pooled and used to the advantage of each individual in the network. The validation and challenge that occur in these groups sharpen the perception and hone the intellect. The sense of community that they create for women isolated by race, sex, or both is invaluable. Specific networking needs are many and varied, but the key to an effective network is empowerment of both the individual and the group. One without the other is ineffective and shortsighted.

The structure and terms of the particular network depend on the purpose that it serves. While some networks are formal and public, others work better if they avoid publicity and visibility. On one predominantly white university campus, black women of all levels (staff, faculty, and administrators) quietly formed an invisible network. With no name, no bylaws, and no public agenda, this group was able to respond effectively to the chilling effect of the Bakke and DeFunis rulings on minority enrollment and persistence. Thanks to the key placement of some members, the group was able to anticipate some major policy decisions, and it organized public events in a number of units and departments. By coming together, these women, who normally were isolated in departments and programs across a large university campus, were able to maximize their knowledge and energies. By ignoring customary divisions by status, group members confirmed the value of networking across levels of responsibility — some of its most informed members were secretaries and administrative assistants. At one point, the issue of publicity was raised. One member wanted to publish pictures of the group and to report on its meetings in a campus newsletter. That idea was voted down, because it endangered the network's major purposes — information and indirect influence. The group's collective energy would be diminished by inquiries for information and by others who wished to use the group for their own ends. So, the network remained invisible. From it came lasting contacts and vital information about policy and decision making on that campus.

In contrast, the National Network of Hispanic Women (NNHW), formerly called Hispanic Women in Higher Education, is a formal, structured organization that provides Hispanic women with visible validation and support. It sponsors conferences and seminars and publishes a national newsletter that provides information on Hispanas in education, government, and business. As Sylvia Castillo (1983, p. 1) notes, "the experience of Hispanas in both the academy of higher learning and in corporate America is a very recent experience. Many... were the first-generation scholars and/or educated women." As a public network, NNHW provides information about academic culture and custom and support that can overcome its members' sense of isolation. It identifies role models for Hispanas new to education or young in the profession, and it raises the consciousness of educational leaders about the talents and abilities of its members. It also promotes interaction between aspiring Hispanas and women and men in leadership positions.

The Black Women's Research and Educational Policy Network fills a similar need for black women across the country. This organization, initiated by Patricia Belle-Scott under a grant from the Wellesley Center for Research on Women, held regional conferences on education and public policy issues and published a quarterly newsletter that reported on regional meetings and scholarly activity, analyzed policy initiatives, and reviewed new publications. Now published by the Women's Research and Resource Center at Spelman College, the newsletter includes a calendar of events and an impressive overview of the many activities that women are organizing. One particularly useful feature of both newsletters has been the profiles of outstanding women of color which highlight the educational and career paths of black and Hispanic role models.

Women of color have always had their own networks so that they would have some arena in which their issues could take priority. A network moves and shifts with its members, and a racially homogeneous group can address concerns that may not appear on other agendas. However, women of color also need to be involved with networks in which they may be in the minority to broaden their contacts and extend their base of information. As participants in these networks, they can influence agendas and strengthen the coalitions among black, Hispanic, Asian, Native American, and white women.

If empowerment is to become real, women must build collaborative networks that recognize and support individual diversity while maximizing collective strength on essential issues. History yields too few instances of such cooperation. However, the three-day International Women's Year Conference in Houston in November 1977 was the site of one spectacularly successful network. The objectives were tough, the stakes were high, and the time was limited. The minority women's plank, part of a National Plan of Action to be adopted at the conference, was to be replaced by a substitute resolution that had to satisfy a rainbow of women delegates: black women from almost every state and territory; Hispanic women, including Chicanas, Puerto Ricans, Cubans, and other Latinas; an Asian American caucus of Chinese Americans, Japanese Americans, Philippinas, and others; Native Americans from many different tribes as well as Alaskan natives; and Pacific Americans from Hawaii, Guam, Samoa, and other trust territories.

Furthermore, the substitute resolution had to get to the convention floor and be submitted to a vote. For this to take place, behind-the-scenes negotiations were necessary. This was no small order under the highly structured procedures of convention protocol. In effect, a number of people and groups had to cooperate, yet the deeply felt issues of each group had to be heard and included. At all-night sessions, in earnest, sometimes heated discussions, each ethnic group aired its issues. Painstakingly, their members discovered that they shared the same issues, although specific experiences and histories had been different. "When the resulting statement was finally read on the conference floor by members of each major caucus. . . many felt it to be the most significant event of Houston and of all that had preceded it. For the first time, minority women—many of whom had been in the leadership of the women's movement precisely because of their greater political understanding of discrimination—were present in such a critical mass that they were able to define their own needs as well as to declare their stake in each women's issue. They were also able to make the media aware of their importance and to forge their own internal networks and coalitions in a way that was far-reaching, inclusive, and an historic 'first' for their communities, for women, and men" (National Commission on the Observance of International Women's Year, 1978, p. 157).

The final moment was electrifying as Maxine Waters, a black assemblywoman from California, was recognized by the chair to introduce the substitute resolution. After she read the umbrella statement applying to all minorities, she yielded to Billie Nave Masters, who had helped other Native American women to prepare for this meeting. Then, Mariko Tse, a young Japanese American actress, spoke for Asian Pacific and Asian American women. She was followed by Sandy Serrano Sewell, president of the Comision Femenil Mexicana, who stood in symbolic unity with Hispanic women from Cuba and Puerto Rico. And finally, Coretta Scott King read the concluding statement on black women.

Taking a cue from the idea of separate and interlocking networks, the National Identification Program for Women in Higher Education Administration, sponsored by the Office of Women at the American Council on Education, has established the most visible network of women administrators in the country. Because its primary purpose is to increase the number of women presidents in colleges and universities, the program has focused on women who already occupy middle- to upper-level administrative positions—a choice that limits severely the number of women of color who can participate. However, this network has taken two steps to involve minority women: It has sponsored networking activities for minority women in the pipeline whose positions and experience do not always suggest the depth and quality of their abilities, and it has established an interlocking network, Focus on Minority Women, that involves regional coordinators and consultants in organizing minority women administrators and addressing advancement issues that concern them.

While networks of one kind or another are essential to individual survival and advancement, the primary purpose of networks for minority women (and, I should hope, for all women) should be to bring about policies and decisions that allow the most able minds of each race and sex to engage the critical issues of the day. An excellent model for achieving this end was described by Gloria Scott, vice-president of Clark College, in a speech that concluded a recent conference sponsored by the Women's Research and Resource Center of Spelman College. Using the human body as a metaphor, Scott (1983, pp. 21, 41) advised minority women to learn from the superb organization and efficiency of the human nervous system: "Networking is about organizing the way impulses and messages are sent, the pathways over which they will be sent before they hit the target, which is some form of expected behavior." The human body has a nerve center that helps to track impulses, determines the desired response, and sends a message through the most efficient pathway. So it is, Scott argued, with networking: "If we are truly interested in making an impact on social policy, then [we must develop] nerve centers that we control and we target."

The early support systems that provided minority families with bed and board in their travels throughout the United States laid the foundation for a network that enabled people of color to challenge custom and discriminatory laws and eventually to bring about the passage of public accommodations legislation. The woman who welcomed to her table the friend of a relative whom she had never seen did not necessarily know that she was a participant in a larger social drama, but she had faith that her individual action somehow helped to advance her people. Lifting as she climbed, she and many like her became the backbone of a civil rights movement that continues to change this country.

The changes that we still seek in the 1980s may not come in our lifetime, and they will not come in response to mere personal ambition. Our collective and individual future lies in how well we network, how committed we are to lifting as we climb, and how well we can pave the way for the next generation of women and men who will work to bring about structural change and to empower women of color.

References

Castillo, S. "Round Table Seminars with Business, Corporate, Government, and Higher Education." *Intercambios Femeniles: A Newsletter of the National Network of Hispanic Women,* 1983, *1* (9), 1. Available by writing to P.O. Box 4223, Stanford, Calif. 94305.

Darden, N.J., and Darden, C. *Spoonbread and Strawberry Wine: Recipes and Reminiscences of a Family.* New York: Anchor Press, 1978.

66

Metha, A. "Networking: A Model for Change." *Journal of National Association of Women Deans, Administrators, and Counselors,* 1979, 31.

National Commission on the Observance of International Women's Year. *The Spirit of Houston: The First National Women's Conference, An Official Report to the President, the Congress, and the People of the United States.* Washington, D.C.: National Commission on the Observance of International Women's Year, 1978.

Scott, G. "Networking: The Impact of Women on Policy Makers When Race, Gender, Class, and Caste Are Variables." *Spelman Messenger,* 1983, *98* (4), 21, 41.

Margaret B. Wilkerson is associate professor in the Department of Afro-American Studies at the University of California at Berkeley and former director of the university's Center for the Study, Education, and Advancement of Women.

Senior women administrators can use their influence over resources to realize existing institutional priorities, but they can also use it to undertake new priorities.

An Agenda for Senior Women Administrators

Sheila Kaplan
Dorothy O. Helly

Virginia Woolf (1966 [1938]) begins her essay "Three Guineas" by addressing a correspondent whose letter has lain upon her conscience for three years. An educated man had written to ask her how she believed that their country could prevent war. The unanswered letter continued to disturb her because, Woolf says, it was "perhaps unique in the history of human correspondence, since when before has an educated man asked a woman how in her opinion war can be prevented?" (p. 3).

Woolf notes that, among the educated classes to which she and the letter writer belong, the historical fact is that families educated sons, not daughters. The result is that "though we see the same world, we see it through different eyes" (p. 18). It took the daughters of England one hundred and fifty years, she says, to earn even a partial franchise and the right to earn, if not a guinea, then a sixpenny bit. There continue to be vast differences between educated men and women as a result of men's long-standing right to education and ownership of land, capital, and patronage. This gulf creates real differences of consciousness as well.

Woolf's insights of almost a half century ago remain pertinent for us today. Although women in the United States are now a large and growing proportion of the college-educated population, we still have not achieved equal

A. Tinsley, C. Secor, S. Kaplan, (Eds.). *Women in Higher Education Administration.*
New Directions for Higher Education, no. 45. San Francisco: Jossey-Bass, March 1984.

access to power and decision making. This lack of equity remains our unfinished agenda.

Its faults and shortcomings notwithstanding, the American university remains a vitally important social institution. As an accepted locus of ideas and ideals, the university seeks to nurture an intellectual environment in which individuals are challenged and encouraged to seek new truths and create new realities. Furthermore, as a community of individuals committed to free inquiry, the university has an obligation to recognize talent and ability and to succor the new and the controversial.

At the same time, universities are very traditional and conservative organizations that accept and accommodate change slowly and grudgingly. It took considerable prodding from the government during the 1970s to make universities commit themselves to affirmative action and the advancement of women. At the highest administrative rank — president or chancellor — women currently serve as the chief executive officers of only 253 institutions, approximately 9 percent of the national total (Office of Women, ACE, 1984). Nevertheless, progress is noticeable. The number of women presidents and chancellors has nearly doubled in the last eight years. In addition, a significant cadre of highly skilled and experienced women who currently hold the position of dean, vice-president, or vice-chancellor will be ready to assume the position of executive officer in the coming years.

Despite such real and measurable advances, the different way in which women and men continue to be socialized and the differences in their access to power and wealth still create differences in their perceptions of the world. Even as women begin to be leaders of colleges and universities in greater numbers, they bring to these roles a sensitivity to their differences with male colleagues in predominantly male academic communities. The desire to fit in, to be seen not as a token but as part of the system, balances the awareness that, whatever they do, they will be seen as representatives of their kind.

As women obtain leadership positions in colleges and universities, do they have a special obligation to take the lead in eschewing the exclusionary practices that characterize society to encourage the advancement of other women? We think that they do. The challenge is to determine the appropriate agenda to be pursued and to develop effective ways of achieving this at reasonable personal cost.

Women who become senior administrative officers are experienced, knowledgeable, and politically astute. They have to be. Climbing to the top of the "greasy pole" — as it was described by the nineteenth-century British prime minister Benjamin Disraeli — is not an easy task, considering the obstacles to be overcome.

The search committees that seek senior administrators are usually composed of senior males. Many of these men are free from overt sexism. Nevertheless, they are often more concerned about the ability of a woman candidate to fit in with the existing organization than they are about her skills,

accomplishments, and vision. Will she work as a member of the team? Can she relate to the male political structure in the community and the region? Can she associate with the local service clubs? Does she like sports, and can she raise money for the football team? Will she be able to work with members of the board of trustees? Can she relate to local political leaders? None of these questions or concerns relate directly to the managerial skills necessary to function effectively as a senior administrative officer. They do reflect, however, the desire of those in universities to be led by individuals who share the organization's values and who can relate to the institution's political, economic, and social realities.

Because male attitudes and values circumscribe and dominate most of the university's environment, women who rise to leadership positions must be comfortable working in such surroundings. Furthermore, a woman must be able to convince male colleagues that her leadership will not undermine the norms of the institution. To meet her professional and personal responsibilities, a senior woman administrator must be comfortable with herself and with her values and yet adaptable enough to accept and operate within the sometimes alien surroundings. At the same time, she should have a clear sense that changes can be made in the institution and its environment.

Women make significant personal sacrifices in the process of climbing the greasy pole. Senior administrators are peripatetic. They must be prepared to move themselves and their families to a new location if they wish to advance professionally. For married women, this need for mobility can have negative effects on husband and family. For unmarried women, moving to another city or town disrupts relationships and personal support groups. Nevertheless, for women who believe that higher education matters and that they can help it to improve, the personal sacrifice becomes tolerable.

Change comes slowly to the university. Traditions of faculty governance, coupled with the legitimate desire of students, staff, alumni, and interested others to be consulted about changes in institutional policies or directions, argue against rapid and centralized decision making. Senior officers are expected to comprehend and to articulate the institution's priorities and to enable it to meet its stated goals. Thus, many of the priorities of senior administrators are inherited from predecessors and rooted in the history and traditions of their institution.

However, the major responsibility of senior officers is to allocate the financial, physical, and personnel resources of academic institutions. In addition, they control access to information, and they can determine the method of its dissemination throughout the university community. Senior officers — male or female — use their influence over these resources to realize existing institutional priorities, but they can also use these resources to undertake new initiatives and to fashion a consensus for policies and programs that will lead to fundamental change. Most pertinent, senior administrators control access to themselves. Time spent meeting with key faculty members, communication of congratulations or praise, and recognition of individual accomplishment can all be used to set a new agenda and create a climate for the acceptance for new ideas.

According to administrative folklore, any new senior officer starts with a sack of marbles that he or she must use to solve problems and make changes. Each new initiative or unpopular decision costs a marble. When the sack is empty, the administrator must move on. The problem is that the senior officer never knows how many marbles there are in the sack to begin with. Yet, there is no mistaking the shape of the empty sack. The careful and creative administrator must therefore use her supply of marbles thoughtfully lest she spend them all on ordinary difficulties. At the same time, spending all her marbles on controversial matters leaves none for managing the daily strains of academic life. For women, the problem is especially acute, because adjustment to administrative leadership in a traditionally male world already contains built-in strains.

When senior women administrators contemplate their responsibilities, they realize that they devote much of their time to personnel matters. In this they resemble other executives. Peters and Waterman (1982) report that the senior executives of America's best-run companies devote a large proportion of their time to personnel matters. The executives whom these authors interviewed believe that the future of their enterprises rests on the quality of the individuals who are its employees and managers and that senior officers should observe, train, and nurture talented staff. Oversight of personnel actions is an equally critical responsibility of senior officers in colleges and universities. Senior women administrators have a professional responsibility to employ faculty and staff of the highest ability and potential.

Data indicate that a significant and growing cadre of highly trained women are prepared to assume managerial and instructional positions in the university. If an organization is to attract the best employees, it must make every effort to recruit from as large a pool as possible. Senior university officers cannot permit institutional inertia, lethargy, or prejudice to prevent the employment of conscientious and talented women. An activist approach to affirmative action in recruitment of administrative personnel should be high on the agenda of all women senior officers. The best way to move an agenda for women within the university is to increase the number of women and minorities in important administrative positions.

Women senior officers should make it clear to all administrators under their supervision that all managers are expected to actively seek to identify, recruit, and hire qualified women and minority candidates. To make this expectation reality, each manager's progress in reaching this goal should be analyzed as part of the manager's annual evaluation, and this analysis should serve as a basis for decisions regarding salary increases and internal promotions. In addition, senior women administrators should meet the institution's level of expectation themselves by identifying women and minorities for positions at the level of vice-president, dean, and director.

When women candidates apply for middle-level administrative positions, they, like senior women, often find that the search committee is concerned about the ability of women candidates to fit in with the local male-dominated environment. Senior women administrators cannot hope to change every aspect of the recruitment process, nor can they ensure that every part of it will be free from the kind of discrimination that discourages women and minority candidates from applying. They can exercise some supervision, work to set a climate of opinion, and encourage reluctant candidates to come forward, but all these activities are time-consuming, and none guarantees success. Each challenge to the dominant values of the institution—high as this must be on the agenda for women—uses up valuable marbles. Only the real difference that having more women in administrative ranks will bring makes the risk worth the cost.

The hiring of faculty is less easy to affect by direct administrative action. Historically, peer evaluation has served as the basis for faculty employment, and there is understandable reluctance on the part of administrators to interfere directly in that process. However, it is clear that concerns about adaptability are part of the peer process and that they make the question of the candidate's acceptance of the peer group's values as important as the candidate's scholarship and teaching ability. To ensure equal treatment of all candidates and to meet an institutional goal of increasing the number of women faculty members, administrators must use both the stick and the carrot.

Procedurally, the institution's affirmative action officer must oversee the faculty selection process to ensure that appropriate efforts are made to identify and evaluate women and minority candidates fairly. On the rare occasions when it is clear that a department's unwillingness to recommend nonwhite male candidates is the result of bias, it may be necessary for the president or the vice-president to prefer an equally well-qualified female or minority applicant over the choice of the faculty committee. Although such action should not be taken lightly, there will be times when the institution's commitment to affirmative action and to hiring the best candidate must take precedence over the parochial views of a department. If budgetary constraints permit, a less confrontational way of reaching the same goal is to distribute new faculty positions to departments with the provision that the positions be filled by qualified women or minority candidates. According to senior administrators who have used this carrot, departments that historically have decried the lack of qualified nonwhite males in their field have been able to find such individuals to fill newly created positions. The risk in dealing with such matters for senior women administrators cannot be underestimated, but if it is judiciously taken, considerable institutional momentum can be built at the cost of only a few marbles.

The responsibility of senior administrators in the area of personnel goes beyond managers and faculty to support staff. Secretaries, clerks, accountants, data entry operators, buildings and grounds personnel, and skilled tradespeople are also university employees, and senior administrators at public and private institutions can work to establish a climate that helps women and minorities in the support staff to advance. Senior administrators should see to it that women are encouraged to apply for employment outside the traditionally female-dominated classifications. Qualified women can be found to work on buildings and grounds crews and to serve as skilled laborers. Furthermore, women students should have opportunities to work on construction and buildings and grounds crews as summer workers with male colleagues. Many college students need summer employment to finance their education. There is no reason why women students should be denied the opportunity to work as summer laborers.

Aside from encouraging women to adopt nontraditional occupations, senior administrators at public and private institutions should investigate the possibility of a comparable-worth salary plan. National studies have shown that women in female-dominated job classifications are paid less than men in male-dominated classifications. Sex-neutral survey instruments have been developed for various job classifications to determine appropriate pay ranges based on the value to the institution of the job performed (Levin, 1984).

However, the decision to support a comparable-worth salary plan has its risks. If adopted, such a plan would increase the institution's salary obligation to its women employees. Since there is no guarantee that new dollars can be found to meet this cost, the institution may be forced to reallocate existing resources to cover the new liability. Given the limited financial resources of most colleges and universities and the high-priority needs of their instructional programs, it is difficult for a woman administrative officer to identify comparable worth as an issue requiring resolution with internal assets. In public institutions, administrators can indicate their support for such plans to legislators and members of the executive branch and work on behalf of a special appropriation designated for this purpose. Because of the financial implications of the comparable-worth issue, the cost to the woman administrator is high.

The obligation of senior women administrators to recognize and support women's concerns and women's perspectives extends beyond personnel and salary policies to the curriculum. For almost a decade and a half, new scholarship on women has been reshaping traditional fields of inquiry and creating the academic discipline of women's studies, and it is becoming increasingly important to integrate this new scholarship on women into existing courses and to provide students with a gender-balanced curriculum. Senior women administrators need to tread carefully here to facilitate without arousing resistance. Identification and support of faculty prepared to work on introducing new scholarship on women into the curriculum is crucial. Women's studies programs need direct and indirect support: Funding is basic, but help in grant writing, prize giving, and sponsored lectureships can also help programs to gain visibility and reputation within the academic community. Women who choose to teach and do research on subjects involving women need to have that choice understood as legitimate when retention, promotion, and tenure decisions are made. Senior women administrators must convey that message to personnel committees in every way that they can.

Another area in which senior women administrators must be conscious of special need is appropriate support programs for both residential and commuter students. The increase in the adult student population since the 1960s has reshaped many college campuses. As the number of women returning to school after marriage and establishing a family — or after divorce and single parenthood — increases, new types of support programs must be created. The need for childcare on campus, including drop-in centers for last-minute baby-sitting problems, remains urgent and unmet in the majority of universities. Coeducational college campuses need women's centers for women of both traditional and nontraditional age — places that can offer individual and group counseling, self-help support groups, and emergency information about all kinds of problems, ranging from rape and wife battering to sexual harrassment. New approaches to career exploration and planning are also important for older women students (Campbell, 1973)

Given today's limited budgets, designing programs and services for adult women will probably require reallocation of resources from existing activities. Since every program or service creates its own interest group, a decision to reduce or eliminate an activity will produce opposition and controversy. A decision to phase out the office of veterans affairs to start a daycare center is certain to cause headlines in the student newspaper and headaches for senior administrators. Yet, in a world of limited budgets, such decisions may be the only way of accommodating a growing sector of the student body.

New monies can be brought in for new needs: if an administrator has initiative and contacts. Every senior woman administrator must be aware of the possibilities of raising funds from private donors, foundations, and federal and state agencies. One of the most interesting phenomena of the last decade is the increase in the number of women administrators in the world of non-profit foundation giving. Many of these women share the agenda for institutional change that we describe here. The relationship can help to return a few marbles to the sack.

The obligation of senior administrators to advance the cause of women reaches beyond the confines of the university into the surrounding community. Most colleges and universities are located in small towns or cities where the institution itself is a major factor in the local economy. By its presence, the institution enhances the quality of life in the region, and it is an important factor in attracting new business and industry. Because the university is so important to the community, its senior officers are usually accorded a privileged place in the local social hierarchy. Membership on boards of directors and chamber of commerce committees is expected of university officers. Senior women officers are particularly in demand when these usually all-male groups make some efforts at integration.

Civic organizations are influential in small towns. Chamber of commerce committees, study groups appointed by a city council, and advisory panels convened by the mayor or city manager play an important role in establishing local priorities. Membership on such bodies is usually reserved for wealthy and influential male members of the community. Although the gender make up of small-town power structures will not change any faster than it does in academic communities, the few women permitted to participate in either setting have a special opportunity to address issues that concern all women. The problem is to speak for women without being typecast or becoming a one-issue person and, as a result, losing influence and credibility.

The major difference between small town and big city for senior women administrators is one of scale and choice. In a large metropolitan area, senior women are still in demand for committees and commissions, platform appearances, and opening addresses, but they can afford to say no more often. In a larger area, they sometimes have an opportunity to deal with educational issues on a scale that affects the lives of many women on many campuses. There are also possibilities for working out an agenda for women with women outside the academic community.

On what terms shall we join the procession of educated men? Virginia Woolf asked. In this chapter, we have laid out a detailed, ambitious agenda for today's senior women administrators and their successors. Transforming this agenda into institutional priorities will not be an easy task. Clearly, administrators who undertake the kind of agenda that would make real institutional change for women possible face great risks. Some institutional positions increase or decrease the risks for individual careers, but eventually all the marbles will be gone from the sack. Despite the difficulties, the stakes for the future of women in higher education are high, and the benefits of even partial success are worth the risks. In university administration, as in all other professions, an enormous sense of personal accomplishment accompanies success, particularly when the venture has been risky. If Woolf was correct — and we believe that she was — senior women administrators must accept the challenge.

References

Blake, R. *Disraeli.* New York: Doubleday, 1967.

Campbell, J. W. "Women Drop Back In: Educational Innovation in the Sixties." In A. Rossi and A. Calderwood (Eds.), *Academic Women on the Move.* Russell Sage Foundation, 1973.

Levin, T. "A New Push to Raise Women's Pay." *New York Times.* January 1, 1984, p. 18.

Peters, T. J., and Waterman, R. H., Jr. *In Search of Excellence: Lessons from America's Best-Run Companies.* New York: Harper & Row, 1982.

Woolf, V. *Three Guineas.* New York: Harcourt Brace Jovanovich, 1966 [1938].

Sheila Kaplan, former vice-president for academic affairs at Winona State University and former director of the City University of New York baccalaureate program, is vice-chancellor for academic affairs in the Minnesota State University system.

Dorothy O. Helly, associate professor of history at Hunter College, is on leave as an ACE Fellow in Academic Administration in the Office of Academic Affairs, City University of New York.

The most promising strategies for the advancement of women in administrative careers focus on efforts to improve mobility in higher education generally.

Foundation Support for Administrative Advancement: A Mixed Record

Alison R. Bernstein

After more than a decade of effort in affirmative action, the number and distribution of women and minority administrators in American colleges and universities have changed very little. For a few highly visible women educators, there has been some improvement. In 1973, Patricia Graham noted that no woman was president of a major coeducational university. Eleven years later, we can identify a handful of women presidents of major institutions and women chancellors of state university systems. However, for the vast majority of women, the long climb up the administrative ladder has not become dramatically easier, despite more than a decade of efforts by private foundations to support projects designed to improve opportunities for advancement by women and minorities in higher education administration.

In the last fifteen years, several major foundations have worked with women and minority educators to address this problem. In 1970, both the Ford Foundation and the Carnegie Corporation began to focus resources on the problem created by underrepresentation of women in higher education leadership positions. The Danforth and Donner Foundations and the Lilly Endowment also sought ways of enhancing opportunities for women and minorities in academic administration. Both Carnegie and Ford, with several

A. Tinsley, C. Secor, S. Kaplan, (Eds.). *Women in Higher Education Administration.*
New Directions for Higher Education, no. 45. San Francisco: Jossey-Bass, March 1984.

smaller foundations, have provided more than $3 million to support projects designed to promote administrative advancement. This figure is drawn from unpublished documents at the Ford Foundation and from annual reports of the Carnegie Corporation for 1976–1982. It represents a conservative estimate because it is based on projects that work specifically on administrative advancement. Thus, the Association of American Colleges' Project on the Status of Women, which received $1 million, has not been included.

The projects that have been funded and the strategies that they have employed have had mixed results, and their success has been limited. Women still constitute less than 15 percent of the chief academic officers in colleges and universities, and most of these women are employed either at small liberal arts colleges and community colleges or in the lower ranks of prestigious research universities. Women remain concentrated in such fields as education, social service, student affairs, and nursing. The distribution of minority administrators in nonminority institutions resembles that of women, but minority participation is even smaller—5 percent of the total (National Advisory Committee on Black Higher Education, 1980). Moreover, for minority administrators who are frequently concentrated in affirmative action positions, upward administrative mobility seems even less possible.

In view of the situation just outlined, this chapter will address three questions: What objectives and strategies did foundations promote to address the problem of administrative advancement for women and minorities? In what ways did these strategies succeed or fail? Do new and different approaches hold even greater potential for change?

From the outset, I must state my belief that the inability of past strategies to solve the problem of administrative advancement was due not to failure of project staff or project design but to underestimation of the degree of structured organizational resistance to any kind of change. Like many other reform measures, the projects funded with outside support helped certain individuals to advance, but they did not alter the broad organizational practices that created the inequities.

Several key objectives guided foundations such as Ford and Carnegie as they sought to improve opportunities for women and minorities in higher education administration. One objective emerged from a concern that the success of legal affirmative action requirements depended on voluntary efforts to increase the pool of minority and women candidates (Ford Foundation, 1974; Carnegie Corporation, 1980). Without priming the pump, as the practice came to be called, it was feared that college and university search committees would ignore the legislative mandate to find qualified women and minority candidates. The second objective grew out of a concern for excellence. Foundations argued that it was important to find talented women and minorities who could lead colleges and universities because their expertise would strengthen higher education institutions, increase their vitality, and bring new vision. Finally, improving the opportunities for women and minorities in higher education administration was seen as a subset of a larger objective — increasing the ranks of women and minority professional workers. Efforts to increase the number of women and minority higher education administrators were similar in this respect to projects aimed at increasing the number of women attorneys and minority engineers.

All three objectives — backstopping affirmative action, strengthening higher education, and increasing the ranks of professional workers — have given legitimacy to administrative advancement projects. Three strategies have been used to accomplish these objectives: identification, preparation, and promotion. Projects to advance women and minority administrators generally concentrate their attention on one or more of these approaches.

All the major projects to advance women and minority administrators work in an extrainstitutional setting. That is, they do not promote the appointment of women and minority administrators on a single campus. Rather, they are activities or programs with a national, regional, or statewide approach. Their broad focus is due in part to foundation interest in funding high-visibility efforts. Nevertheless, conforming to the funder's expectations is only one reason for the extrainstitutional character of most projects. In general, it is easier to foster change in individual attitudes in a new organizational setting away from a person's home campus than it is to attack the issue of advancement within an existing administrative structure. Thus, whether a project employs an identification or a promotion strategy, it usually operates outside the individual's college or university.

One major project that uses an identification strategy also relies on newly created networks outside colleges and universities to find talented women who are ready to move into senior academic administrative positions. The American Council on Education's National Identification Program (ACE/NIP), which was established in 1977 with a grant from the Carnegie Corporation, now operates in every state. A hallmark of this program, which has received more than $600,000 in foundation support over the last seven years, is its focus on making women better known outside their own campus. ACE/NIP establishes a group of women academic administrators in each state to hold regular meetings and organize conferences on higher education issues. This type of academic women's club is used to create a personalized network of contacts, to learn about job opportunities, and to share work experiences.

The ACE/NIP strategy is based on the premise that many qualified women are ready to assume positions of increased responsibility. However, these women are not known to their female colleagues, and — more important — they are invisible to the existing male leadership network that chooses college and university administrators. The state-based groups serve as talent scouts, identifying and promoting the best and brightest of their members. Once an individual has been so designated, she can be invited to participate in a national forum, where she can interact and discuss issues in higher education with a team of male and female national leaders.

Although a complete evaluation of the first eight years of the ACE/NIP program is still pending, several impressions about the program's effectiveness can be shared. First, there is preliminary evidence that between 20 and 25 percent of its 800 participants have moved into higher positions. Whether this is a direct result of their involvement with ACE/NIP is uncertain. Perhaps these women were already on their way up, and the program merely helped them to get there faster. In any case, ACE/NIP appears to be a successful program, and women seem to be eager to take part in it. However, ACE/NIP has not fundamentally changed the nature of the male-dominated search process. Search committees now have easier access to a pool of qualified women because of ACE/NIP activities, but whether they will adopt this identification model without ACE/NIP assistance is not clear. Moreover, we do not know whether the ACE/NIP model works to improve administrative advancement for women on their own campuses. We do know, however, that ACE/NIP has not challenged the criteria used for selecting senior administrative officers. Rather, it seeks to find women who can meet them. Thus, it works within the existing structures while incrementally attempting to challenge conventional values and prejudices.

Preparing women for increasingly greater administrative responsibility is the second major strategy, which characterizes several projects. It first emerged in a 1970 Ford Foundation grant to support the recruitment of women into the summer training program for senior administrators conducted by the Institute for Educational Management (IEM) at the Harvard Business School. The IEM program was not specifically designed for women, but Ford support enabled the program to recruit sixty-two women administrators between 1970 and 1974. With their more numerous male counterparts, women received training in such subjects as budgeting, information systems, fund raising, endowment management, and governmental relations.

Departing in 1973 from the IEM model, both the Ford Foundation and the Carnegie Corporation made grants to the University of Michigan to establish the first Institute for Administrative Advancement of Academic Women. As its name suggests, the institute was designed for women only, and it provided training for junior faculty women. The institute covered such topics as collective bargaining, legal problems of universities, and personnel management. The Michigan institute led the way for a number of women-only training programs, including the HERS/Bryn Mawr College Summer Institute for Women in Higher Education Administration funded in 1976 by the Donner Foundation, and later the Wellesley weekend seminars in administration supported by the Fund for the Improvement of Post-Secondary Education.

This strategy has proven highly successful both in attracting women participants and in securing funds from the participant's own institution to pay for the training. The eighty women selected each year to participate in the Bryn Mawr program welcome the chance to immerse themselves in a mini-college experience free from family and job responsibilities. For a brief time, they are students again, participating in lectures, discussions, simulations, and case studies, but now they are older, wiser, and eager to make the most of the training experience. The setting itself promotes the goal of helping them to get more out of their professional lives.

Although the Summer Institute has been extremely successful in teaching management skills and in enhancing perspectives, this approach is not without problems. Designed to get women faculty and administrators consciously involved in their own career development, the program focuses on motivating women to seek additional responsibility, not on motivating their supervisors to promote them or on changing the institutions in which they work. This self-help approach may reinforce the expectation that women must do more and learn more than men to get ahead. The onus appears to be on women to perform, not on the system to change.

The third strategy that characterizes advancement programs involves the promotion of women for administrative positions. Promotion entails recruiting women for specific jobs, getting letters of recommendation, helping women to apply for jobs, building support for women candidates, and monitoring the search process. During the 1970s, both Ford and Carnegie made grants to help in establishing regional referral organizations. The first such organization, Higher Education Resources Services (HERS), was developed by a group of women administrators in New England. HERS, New England received its first Ford grant in 1972, and it was housed at Brown University. According to unpublished documents in Ford Foundation archives, its primary goal was to develop facilities for a placement and referral service to assist chairmen and high-level administrators in finding women for academic positions.

Two years later, Ford made a supplemental grant to Brown University to continue the work of HERS, New England and to establish a similar office for the Mid-Atlantic region at the University of Pennsylvania. It is worth noting that several of the women responsible for establishing both HERS offices have themselves moved up the administrative ladder. For example, of the seven women who served on the first advisory committee for HERS, Mid-Atlantic, none held a rank higher than dean. Within a few years, three became presidents, and two assumed more responsible administrative positions. In 1979, a third HERS office was established at the University of Utah to cover the Rocky Mountain region.

At first, the HERS strategy of referring and promoting women for jobs seemed a logical step: a kind of postdoctoral placement service. Hundreds of eager women signed up to become part of the system in each region. Moreover, search committees sought names from HERS offices as a way of demonstrating their commitment to affirmative action. In the early years, there was much enthusiasm about the HERS model. For the first time in higher education, there was a system. Someone was charged with promoting women and with helping them to steer a successful course from learning that a job opening existed to negotiating salaries and benefits.

However, it is one thing to equip women with job-hunting skills and build a network to help them, and it is quite another thing to secure a job. For the most part, HERS was still outside the decision-making process. Once some of the most visible women candidates had moved into chief executive officer positions, the enthusiasm for HERS died down. It proved harder to move the next cohort along. Moreover, women seeking positions began to use their own networks, rather than listing with or relying on HERS. By the end of the 1970s, HERS offices were moving into other forms of service, including conferences and leadership development and training programs for faculty and administrators, trustees, nonprofessional staff, and students. These functions are by no means unimportant, but they indicate that the original mission of HERS has been fundamentally transformed.

I comment critically on each of these strategies — identification, preparation, and promotion — because none has directly challenged the premise that women, rather than institutional practices and the values of the academy, were responsible for the scarcity of female administrative officers. Either women were not visible enough, or they did not have the proper training, or they needed help to secure a job. Certainly, all these statements are true to some degree. However, the problem must be seen from another perspective if we are to develop more effective solutions. Foundations and others must ask, How must the system change so that it can use more women and minority administrators at the highest levels?

Questioning the system focuses on structures, institutions, and entry points for groups of people, not for single individuals. It also forces male administrators to address fundamental problems of the system, not simply to ask women to change their behavior or acquire male skills and training. Unless the broad questions are asked, there is little incentive for males to change a system that has worked for them.

Ironically, the system has not worked equally well for all males. Black male presidents who head historically black colleges remain a segregated leadership group. It is almost as difficult for the chief executive officer of a black institution to become the president of a white institution as it is for the president of a community college — male or female — to assume the presidency of a four-year college. The existing system has also denied administrative advancement opportunities to certain classes of men.

Another barrier to the advancement of women and minorities results from the way in which academic administrators are chosen. Traditionally, academic administrators have emerged from the faculty. More than 80 percent of the administrators who responded to Moore's (1982) survey had held faculty rank, usually at the full or associate professor level. However, in view of the small number of faculty openings projected for the next twenty years, it is not very likely that there will be enough women and minority faculty members to fill administrative posts. Perhaps we should ask whether former faculty members do in fact make the best university administrators. To my knowledge, no study demonstrates that a skilled faculty researcher is also a competent manager. It is simply assumed that someone who comes from the faculty is preferable (for other faculty) to an experienced administrator who has worked in other settings. Perhaps administrators should be selected on the basis of competence, not of previous status. However, our current strategies do not address this issue.

As we search for new strategies to improve administrative advancement opportunities for women and minorities, we must keep institutional, sector, and credential barriers in mind. Data show that it is extremely difficult for a community college administrator to move to a state college or university or to a research university. Mobility is also limited between the public and private sectors. Moreover, individuals who lack standard faculty credentials are often not seriously considered for administrative positions.

In the future, foundations should stimulate interinstitutional and intersector mobility for qualified women and minority male administrators. Particularly among the black colleges, this step might enable black women to move into the traditionally all-male presidential positions. In addition, we should work to revise the criteria and qualifications deemed appropriate for administrative service. Unless we challenge the path that leads from faculty member to academic administrator, we will be only marginally effective in advancing opportunities for large numbers of women and minority males in the next twenty years.

Strategies to address the twin issues of increased mobility and improved credentials will not only affect women and minorities, they will also affect the administrative advancement of men who have not been able to secure tenured positions or who have worked in only one kind of academic institution, such as a community college. Because these issues touch fundamental structural and personnel relationships in higher education, they should not be viewed exclusively as equity issues. Rather, they are improvement issues that go beyond projects for special populations. In a period of increasing political conservatism and academic retrenchment, arguments to improve the overall quality of colleges and universities are more likely to generate foundation support than arguments tied exclusively to equity concerns. In other words, the most promising future strategies for administrative advancement will focus on institutional improvement, not on individual gain.

References

Carnegie Corporation. Annual Report. New York: Carnegie Corporation, 1980.

Ford Foundation. "That 51 Percent: Ford Foundation Activities Related to Opportunities for Women." Ford Foundation Report. New York: Ford Foundation, 1974.

Ford Foundation. Unpublished document describing HERS, New England goals, 1972.

Graham, P. "Status Transition of Women Students, Faculty, and Administrators." In A. Rossi and A. Calderwood (Eds.), *Academic Women on the Move.* New York: Russell Sage Foundation, 1973.

Moore, K. M. *Leaders in Transition: A National Study of Higher Education Administrators.* University Park, Penn.: Center for the Study of Higher Education, Pennsylvania State University, 1982.

National Advisory Committee on Black Higher Education and Black Colleges and Universities. *Needed Systems Supports for Achieving Higher Education Equity for Black Americans: A Synthesis Document.* Washington, D.C.: U.S. Government Printing Office, 1980.

Alison R. Bernstein is program officer in the Education and Culture Program at the Ford Foundation and a former program officer of the Fund for the Improvement of Post-Secondary Education.

The insights and innovations of the 1970s must be institutionalized and emerging issues must be addressed.

Getting the Best: Conclusions, Recommendations, and Selected Resources

Sheila Kaplan
Cynthia Secor
Adrian Tinsley

The chapters in this sourcebook have described current research on the career paths of women administrators, successful networking and intervention strategies, and appropriate agendas for senior administrators and foundation officers. Yet, we are less than sanguine about the degree to which commitment to the advancement of women and minorities has been institutionalized by American higher education. The phrases *affirmative action* and *equal opportunity* have been in use for such a long time that we sometimes appear to have lost the focus on action and opportunity. While some progress has been made, action on equity issues does not appear to be high on the agenda of our profession.

As we and others in this sourcebook have stated, senior administrators must be concerned about expanding the number of talented women and minorities who serve their institutions. Those who are not are wasting an enormous reservoir of talent and denying their institutions the creativity and vision that new ideas and values can bring. Furthermore, we are convinced

A. Tinsley, C. Secor, S. Kaplan, (Eds.). *Women in Higher Education Administration.*
New Directions for Higher Education, no. 45. San Francisco: Jossey-Bass, March 1984.

that all who serve higher education have a right both to meaningful work and to meaningful careers. Each of us, irrespective of gender, has the right to participate in the leadership and management of higher education and to have our expertise and wisdom guide developments within our profession.

At least twelve strategies must be followed to support the advancement of women and minorities in higher education administration. The success of these strategies will depend on the willingness of individual administrators to take specific and identifiable action that will advance women and minorities. First, administrators must make affirmative action and the advancement of women and minorities a publicly stated personal and institutional priority and commitment. Second, administrators must recognize and promote the value of the diverse styles and values that the addition of women and minorities to management will introduce. Third, administrators should make recruitment and employment of women and minorities a job requirement for subordinates and make successful accomplishment of this goal an important part of performance evaluation and salary review. Fourth, administrators should make themselves aware of current research on women and minorities and its potential impact on the policies and practices of their institution. Fifth, administrators should make themselves aware of the different career paths of women and men administrators within their institutions and devise ways of removing the gender-linked barriers. Sixth, administrators should encourage and support women's and minority advocacy groups on campus and, where appropriate, incorporate their ideas into institutional policy and practices. Seventh, administrators should encourage the mentoring of promising women and minorities and be prepared to demonstrate personal willingness to sponsor and advance someone quite different from themselves. Eighth, administrators must recognize that women and minorities who are seeking the skills to become senior managers need specialized training. Assistance should be provided in the form of on-campus professional development programs, financial and other support for attendance at nationally recognized residential training programs, development of on-campus internship opportunities in administration, and development of career ladder programs that highlight promotional opportunities within the institution. Ninth, administrators should educate the members of their board of trustees to the importance of affirmative action to the health and vitality of the institutions that they govern and seek board support and assistance in the advancement of women and minorities. Tenth, administrators who serve on national, regional, state, or local commissions or study groups should raise issues of concern to women and minorities that it is appropriate for the group to address. One does not have to be a woman or a minority person to raise these issues; sometimes they are best raised by a white male. Eleventh, administrators should choose to serve on national, regional, and state commissions and task forces set up to deal with the concerns of women and minorities. Last, administrators should continue the pressure on professional associations to keep concerns about women and minorities high on the agenda. Professional associations are in a unique position to serve as clearing-houses for policies and practices that have been successful in advancing women and minorities.

Emerging Issues

As we look ahead to the end of the century, we see five issues emerging that the higher education profession must recognize and address. First, the commitment to and support for the advancement of women and minorities that characterized the rhetoric of the late 1970s and that resulted in substantial gains seems to have diminished. Although women's issues and minority concerns are assuming a higher profile in local and national political arenas, the same cannot be said for the higher education arena. Data show that nearly 80 percent of the newly created administrative positions are filled by white males (Dingerson and others, 1980). At the same time, women and minorities comprise a growing majority of the consumers of higher education. It is evident that more intervention strategies need to be crafted to increase the number of women and minority administrators.

Second, the development, testing, and dissemination of intervention strategies cost money. Support from the government and from private foundations underwrote the networking, mentoring, and training programs of the 1970s. Programs that have been unable to become self-supporting have vastly scaled back their activities, and their visibility has declined. The issue of where money to support a new generation of strategies and programs will come from is crucial and must be addressed.

Third, a great deal of research in the past few years has focused on women in management. While such research is interesting in itself, it does not easily yield information that can be used to shape institutional policies and practices that support the advancement of women and minorities. What are needed are longitudinal studies of women and men, both majority and minority, in different types of institutions and in different regions of the country that will yield detailed information about the factors that promote and hinder advancement. Much of this research could be undertaken by individual institutions as part of their routine information gathering if there were national agreement on the factors to be studied and on the methodology to be used.

Fourth, for the economic and political implications of gender, comparable worth is perhaps the single most important issue on the horizon. If the effort and intelligence expended on work is rewarded for its centrality to the shared enterprise, the entire reward structure of the institution will change and with it the perceived status structure. Depending on one's point of view, this is either exhilarating or unnerving.

Fifth, the gains made by women and minorities owe much to a small, hardworking, dedicated, and driven cadre of leaders and advocates who make the cause of these groups their own. Enormous amounts of creative energy and talent were invested, often with meager financial reward. Many of these individuals have moved on to other stages in their careers. Thus, it is imperative that a new generation of leaders emerge. It is not clear, however, where they will come from.

Conclusion

The advances that women and minorities have made in higher education administration in the past decade have come slowly, painfully, and grudgingly. They are fragile, and they can easily be eroded or erased. To prevent such slippage, the insights and innovations of the 1970s must be carefully evaluated and safely institutionalized while new agendas are prepared to address emerging issues and challenges. A new generation of leaders must be identified, and funds must be provided to support programs and activities to assist women and minorities.

Faced with this awesome task and with so much yet to be done, we must retain our commitment both to the importance of that task and to the possibility of accomplishing it. Progress will be incremental. We can with confidence look forward to a time when higher education professionals will automatically and unself-consciously take into account the impact of gender and ethnic or racial status on all the programs and policies with which they deal. This time will come most quickly if we all — in our own persons and as representatives of the educational institutions from which our authority derives — strive to create and maintain a higher education establishment that reflects the American people as a whole.

Selected Resources*

Organizations

ACE National Identification Program (ACE/NIP)
Office of Women in Higher Education
American Council on Education
Suite 829, Dupont Circle
Washington, D.C. 20036
(202) 833-4692
Donna Shavlik, Director

American Association of Women in Community and Junior Colleges
American Association of Community and Junior Colleges

---

*Adapted and condensed from a comprehensive resource list prepared by Judy Touchton, associate director of the Office of Women in Higher Education, American Council on Education, with the assistance of Caroline Russe, and available at cost from the Office of Women in Higher Education, ACE.

Suite 410, 1 Dupont Circle
Washington, D.C. 20036
(202) 293-7050
Carol Eliason, Director of Special Projects

Association of Black Women in Higher Education
30 Limerick Drive
Albany, New York 12204
(518) 465-2146
Jacqueline A. Kane, Conference Committee Chairperson

Higher Education Resource Services (HERS), New England
Cheever House, Wellesley College
Wellesley, Massachusetts 02181
(617) 235-0320, ext. 2529
Lilli Hornig, Director

Higher Education Resources Services (HERS), Mid-America
University of Denver, Colorado Women's College Campus
Denver, Colorado 80220
(303) 394-6866
Cynthia Secor, Director

Higher Education Resources Services (HERS), West
293 Union Building, University of Utah
Salt Lake City, Utah 98412
(801) 581-3745
Shauna Adix, Director

Hispanic Higher Education Coalition
Suite 200, 1725 Eye Street, NW
Washington, D.C. 20006
(202) 638-1339
Raphael Magellan, President

Intercambios Femeniles
Stanford University
Stanford, California 94304
(415) 497-2733
Sylvia Castillo, Assistant Director of Student Affairs

National Association for Women Deans, Administrators, and Counselors
Suite 210, 1325 Eighteenth Street, NW
Washington, D.C. 20006
(202) 659-9330
Patricia Rueckel, Executive Director

National Chicano Council on Higher Education
Suite 201, 600 W. Twenty-eighth Street
Austin, Texas 78705
(512) 479-8497

National Council for Research on Women
474 E. Sixty-fifth Street
New York, New York 10021
Mary Ellen Capek, Executive Secretary

New England Minority Women's Association
University of Massachusetts
Amherst, Massachusetts 01003
Marie Reid, President

Project on the Status and Education of Women
Association of American Colleges
1818 R Street, NW
Washington, D.C. 20009
(202) 387-1300
Bernice R. Sandler, Director

Data and Statistics

Frances, C., and Mensel, R. F. *Women and Minorities in Administration of Higher Education Institutions: Employment Patterns and Salary Comparisons 1978–79 and an Analysis of Progress Toward Affirmative Action Goals 1975–76 and 1978–79.* Washington, D.C. College and University Personnel Association, 1981. Available for fee from College and University Personnel Association, 11 Dupont Circle, Washington, D.C. 20036

Howard, S. *But We Will Persist: A Comparative Research Report on the Status of Women in Academia.* Washington, D.C.: American Association of University Women, 1978.

Moore, K. M. *Leaders in Transition: A National Study of Higher Education Administrators.* University Park, Penn.: Center for the Study of Higher Education, Pennsylvania State University, 1982. Summary and selected monographs are available at cost from the Center for the Study of Higher Education, 324 Pond Laboratory, Pennsylvania State University, University Park, Pennsylvania 16802. Monographs include *On Presidents, Provosts, and Deans' Careers* and *Women and Minorities.*

Shavlik, D., and Touchton, J. *Women Chief Executive Officers in College and Universities, Table VIII.* Washington, D.C.: Office of Women in Higher Education, American Council on Education, 1984.

Wilson, R., and Melendez, S. E. *Minorities in Higher Education: Second Annual Status Report.* Washington, D.C.: Office of Minority Concerns, American Council on Education, 1983.

Technical Assistance

Higher Education Salary Evaluation Kit. American Association of University Professors, 1 Dupont Circle, Washington, D.C. 20036.

Institutional Self-Study Guide. Project on the Status and Education of Women, Association of American Colleges, 1818 R Street, NW, Washington, D.C. 20036.

Resource Directory: Organizations and Publications that Promote Sex Equity in Post-secondary Education, 1982. Project on the Status and Education of Women, Association of American Colleges, 1818 R Street, NW, Washington, D.C. 20036.

Geis, F. L., Carter, M. R., and Butler, D. J. *Seeing and Evaluating People.* Newark: University of Delaware, 1982. Research report on perception and perceptual stereotypes (84 pp.) or summary (20 pp.) available on request from Office of Women's Affairs, University of Delaware, Newark, Delaware 19711.

Reference

Dingerson, M. R., Rodman, J. A., and Wade, J. F. "The Hiring of Academic Administrators Since the 1972 Higher Education Guidelines." *Research in Higher Education,* 1980, *13,* 9–22.

Sheila Kaplan, former vice-president for academic affairs at Winona State University and former director of the City University of New York baccalaureate program, is vice-chancellor for academic affairs in the Minnesota State University System.

Cynthia Secor, founding director of HERS, Mid-Atlantic, which for many years was based at the University of Pennsylvania, continues in this role with HERS, Mid-America, which is based at the University of Denver. She is cofounder and codirector of the Summer Institute for Women in Higher Education Administration.

Adrian Tinsley, associate vice-chancellor for academic affairs in the Minnesota State University System, designed the professional development unit for the Bryn Mawr/HERS Summer Institute for Women in Higher Education Administration, where she serves as faculty in residence.

Index

A

Adix, S., 89

Administrative Skills Program, 3; analysis of, 35–45; described, 35–36; discussion of, 42–45; evaluation of, 37–38; findings from, 38–43; goals of, 36; and networking, 36, 44–45

Administrators: age of, 11–12; career issues for, 7; careers of, 5–15; current position by race and sex of, 6–7; demographics on, 6–9; doctoral education of, 12–13; educational backgrounds of, 9; as first holders of position, 7–8; by institutional types, 8; and length of time in current position, 8; marital status of, 12; personal backgrounds of, 9; personal characteristics of, 11–13; professional backgrounds of, 6; and spouses' occupations, 9; spouses of, as volunteers, 56. *See also* Women administrators

Affirmative action, and senior women administrators, 70–71

American Association of Community and Junior Colleges, 88–89

American Association of University Professors, 91

American Association of University Women, 26

American Association of Women in Community and Junior Colleges, 88–89

American Council on Education (ACE), 5, 47–48, 53, 54, 56, 57, 58, 88; Commission on Women in Higher Education of, 47–49; Office of Women in Higher Education (OWHE) of, 2, 3, 47, 48, 49, 51, 52, 53, 56, 57, 64, 68, 74, 88. *See also* National Identification Program

Association of American Colleges, Project on the Status and Education of Women, 2, 78, 90, 91

Association of Black Women in Higher Education, 89

Astin, H. S., 48, 58

B

Bakke ruling, 62

Belle-Scott, P. 63

Bennett, S. K., 17, 24

Bernstein, A. R., 3–4, 77–84

Black Women's Research and Educational Policy Network, 63

Blake, R., 74

Brown, L. K., 44–45

Brown University, HERS, New England at, 81

Bryn Mawr College, Summer Institute at, 3, 18, 25, 27, 80

Butler, D. J., 91

C

Campbell, J. W., 73, 74

Capek, M. E., 17, 24, 45, 57, 58, 90

Career mapping: concept of, 19; individual and organizational factors in, 19–20; and next significant job, 22; outcomes of, 23–24; and professional development, 17–24; situational questions for, 21; value of, 22–23; value questions for, 21, 22

Career tracks, issue of, 7

Careers: analysis of, 5–15; background on, 5–6; barriers in, 19, 49, 82–83; conclusion on, 14; defined, 9; demographics of, 6–9; elements defining, 9–11; issues in, 7; organizational factors in, 13–14; personal characteristics shaping, 11–13; responsibility, recognition, and reward in, 11

Carnegie Code Classification System, 8

Carnegie Commission, 26, 33

Carnegie Corporation of New York, 1n, 48, 53, 54, 77–78, 79, 80, 81, 83

Carter, M. R., 91

Castillo, S., 63, 65, 89

College and University Personnel Association, 90

Curby, V. M., 12, 14

93